5X YOUR WEALTH

5X YOUR WEALTH

Two Incomes, One Plan to 5X Your Wealth with Australian Property & Shares

A story-driven guide to building lasting wealth as a couple with property and shares.

VICTOR OWI IDOKO

CFA · CFP · SSA · M.Com

CFV Advisory

Level 45, 680 George Street, Sydney NSW, Australia

admin@cfvadvisory.com.au · cfvadvisory.com.au

Printed in the country purchased.

First Edition: 2026

Important Notice

PLEASE READ BEFORE YOU BEGIN

General information only. This book provides general information and education about wealth-building principles and about property and share investing in Australia. It is not personal financial product advice, taxation advice, credit assistance or legal advice, and it must not be relied upon as a substitute for advice that considers your own circumstances.

No personal advice, and no client relationship. Although the author is a licensed financial adviser, in writing this book he is not acting as your adviser and is not providing you with a financial service. Reading this book does not create an adviser–client relationship. Nothing in it has been prepared by reference to your personal objectives, financial situation or needs. The author provides personal financial advice only to his own clients, under a separate written agreement and after considering their individual circumstances.

Get advice that fits your life. Before acting on anything you read here, obtain personal advice from professionals licensed to consider your circumstances: a licensed financial adviser, a registered tax agent or accountant, a credit-licensed mortgage broker and, where relevant, a solicitor. Where any financial product is mentioned, obtain and read the relevant Product Disclosure Statement (PDS) and Target Market Determination (TMD), and consider whether the product is appropriate for you, before making a decision.

Figures and laws change. The rates, thresholds, rules and government settings described in this book - including negative gearing, the capital gains tax discount, franking credits, superannuation contributions and caps, lending rules and interest rates - were current, to the best of the author's knowledge, at the time of writing and are general in nature. Tax and superannuation law changes frequently. Confirm the current position with the ATO, ASIC's Moneysmart, your adviser or your accountant before relying on any figure in these pages.

The stories are real, but anonymised. The case studies are drawn from real experience and have been anonymised. Names, locations, incomes and identifying details have been changed, and some accounts are composites assembled to illustrate a principle. Any resemblance to a specific identifiable person is unintended. The outcomes described are illustrations, not representations of what you can expect.

No guarantees. Past performance is not a reliable indicator of future performance. All investing carries risk, including the risk of losing money; property and share markets fall as well as rise. The title - 5X Your Wealth - describes an illustration of what disciplined, structured investing can do over time. It is not a promise, a forecast of your results, or a guarantee.

Limitation of liability. To the maximum extent permitted by law, the author, CFV Advisory and the publisher exclude all liability for any loss or damage (including indirect or consequential loss) arising from any person acting, or failing to act, on anything contained in this book. Nothing in this notice excludes, restricts or modifies any consumer guarantee, right or remedy under the Australian Consumer Law or any other law that cannot lawfully be excluded.

Victor Owi Idoko provides financial services through CFV Advisory. Authorised Representative No. 001238690.

-•-

Read it slowly. Talk about it together. Then get advice that fits your life.

For the Australian couples who decide, together, what kind of wealth builders they want to be.

Contents

Foreword

BY GODFREY PHILLIPS OAM

Laureate of the Financial Hall of Fame

Victor Idoko and I have a lot in common. He emigrated to Australia to educate himself and to seek the opportunities to build a future he probably could not have had in his former home, Nigeria. I was born in India, and my parents emigrated to Australia to give us three children an opportunity we possibly would not have had there. We both went to boarding schools, which was pivotal in developing discipline, self-reliance, and answering to strict times for prayer, class, sport, and study. This built a solid, principled foundation where a culture of excellence was the accepted norm and mediocrity was not tolerated. We both used these early lessons to build our financial planning businesses - but this is Victor's story.

Victor graduated from the University of Western Australia (UWA), where he completed his Masters and Honours years in Economics, Accounting, and Finance (Investments). These solid foundations were laid to build a career in finance. Victor's vision was to make financial planning accessible, straightforward and simple to understand. His firm, CFV Advisory - a testament to hard work and dedication - grew from this vision, prioritising the client's needs and a client-first approach that quickly set it apart in the industry. Building relationships is the key, and this is gained by asking the right questions to know the client better, which allows Victor to always advise and work in his client's best interest. Victor is a great listener - a very important and mandatory requisite in financial planning.

Victor is a member of the prestigious Million Dollar Round Table (MDRT), the premier global association of financial professionals. As a highly respected Court of the Table member, he belongs to the top 1% of financial planners in the world. He has spoken at the MDRT, which is an honour, and there will be further opportunities to speak and to contribute to leadership committees. His whole-person ethos, a core philosophy he advocates, of finding balance across all areas of life: health, wealth, family, business, spirituality, education and relationships, fits perfectly with the MDRT ethos. Victor is a highly principled professional.

If you want to create wealth with the right structure, preserve that wealth with the correct financial plans in place, and then distribute it tax-effectively at the appropriate time, this book of stories and instruction is for you. Victor will work closely with you to consider your vision and your plans, and to write down meaningful, achievable goals built on good, solid foundations. Resilience and trust over the tough times will be necessary, and Victor will help navigate a successful pathway for you.

Victor's journey from Nigeria to becoming a financial planner in Australia is a story of resilience, strategic thinking, perseverance, commitment to vision, dedication and impact.

Godfrey Phillips OAM
Laureate of the Financial Hall of Fame

Preface

BEFORE WE BEGIN

My parents built their wealth the hardest way possible.

They did it without guidance, without structure, without anyone leaning across a table to tell them what was really going on. They did it in Nigeria, where a currency could lose half its worth while you slept, where the ground beneath your money was never quite still. They worked, and they saved, and they held on, and they did all of it on instinct, because the tools and the guidance in this book were never offered to them.

I have thought a great deal about what their lives might have looked like if they had been advised, if someone had shown them how to place two ordinary assets where the current couldn't reach them, and then simply wait. In that country, in those years, I believe they could have multiplied what they built fifty times over. I know my own life would have been easier for it. I know theirs would have too.

I did not escape the same lesson. Eighteen years ago, holding an investment I didn't fully understand, I grew frightened, and I sold, it was at the wrong moment, for the wrong reason. It cost me more than money; it cost me years. If I could hand a single book back through time to the version of me sitting there with his finger over the button, it would be this one. I write the books I wish I had read.

Here is the truth I most want you to carry in from the first page: the maths of building wealth is easy. It is far simpler than you fear; you will be surprised how simple. The hard part was never the numbers. The hard part is the psychology, the fear that makes you sell, the impatience that makes you chase, the noise that makes you doubt a plan that was working perfectly well. That is the real work of this book, and the good news is that the work can be done. Ordinary people do it every day.

You may feel behind. Most people who pick up a book like this do. I want to give you permission to feel behind - and then to stop caring about it, and to keep moving anyway. Where you begin matters far less than that you begin, and that you don't stop. Structure and momentum beat brilliance every time.

Mostly I work with couples, and I have written this book for two. There is a real advantage in building together - two incomes, two minds, two people to steady each other when one of you wants to jump. But if you are reading this on your own, don't put it down. The principles don't require a partner. They only require that you start.

And once you have started, build for the people you love, not for a number on a screen. Then teach someone else what you learned. Ask for help when you need it - there is no prize for doing this alone, or in the dark. Wealth built patiently, shared generously, and passed on well is the only kind worth the effort.

A few words on how to read what follows.

Read it slowly, and if you can, read it together. Each chapter opens with two people at a real moment, then steps back into history and forward into Australia today. The principle always lives inside the story - you won't need to take notes to feel it land. At the end of each chapter there is one question. Sit with it. Talk it over before you turn the page. The couples who do best with this book are the ones who argue gently over it on a Sunday night, then do one small thing on Monday.

One last thing. When a chapter mentions a tax rule or a figure, remember that it was true when it was written - but the rules change. Check the current position before you lean on it. The principles in this book will outlast the numbers by decades. That is rather the point.

I built the tools I wish my parents had been handed. They're yours now.

Victor Owi Idoko
Sydney, 2026

Two ordinary assets, patiently managed
with discipline and structure, will outperform
almost any clever strategy -
across every era, every market,
and every generation.

INTRODUCTION

Why You Should Build Wealth

Stewardship beats status

It's a Sunday night in Brisbane. Dinner is finished, the kids are in bed, and two people are sitting at the kitchen table with a laptop open between them.

They aren't fighting. Actually, they're doing something quieter and more unsettling than that. They're looking at their finances.

On paper, everything is fine. Between them, they earn good money. They own a home. They have two super accounts sitting somewhere in the background. They are, by most measures, doing well.

But the spreadsheet tells a different story. After the mortgage, the school fees, the car repayments, and the cost of simply running a life in a capital city - there is almost nothing left over. They can't quite work out why. Or what to do about it.

"We should be further ahead than this," one of them says.

The other one doesn't argue.

If that moment sounds familiar - this book was written for you.

***Before this book asks you to do anything, it wants to answer one question that most finance books skip entirely: why build wealth at all? Not how.* Why.**

The Myth

If the *why* isn't right, the *how* won't stick. You'll start strong, lose momentum when life gets in the way, and find yourself back at the same kitchen table twelve months later with the same quiet unease.

Most people, when they're honest about it, have two answers to that question. The first is survival - security, safety, not having to worry. The second is something harder to name. A sense that they're capable of more. That their family deserves more. That the life they can see clearly in their mind is closer than it feels.

Both are valid answers, but only one of them will sustain a 14-year wealth-building plan.

If you noticed, one of the answers above is fear-based. The other is purpose-based. Let me say it straight: Fear of falling behind will get you started. It won't keep you going. Here's why:

The couple building from fear makes decisions designed not to lose. They hold cash because markets might fall. They delay investing because the timing doesn't feel right. They pay down the mortgage at the expense of every other strategy because at least that feels safe. They are playing defence, permanently, and defence, held long enough, becomes its own kind of loss. The money sits. The years pass. The compounding that should have been working quietly in the background never starts.

The couple building from purpose makes a different set of decisions. Not reckless ones - patient ones. They invest when prices are uncomfortable because they know time matters more than timing. They hold when markets fall because selling would mean abandoning the plan, and the plan is bigger than any single quarter. They build the structure, and then they trust it. They are playing offence - not aggressively, but consistently - and consistency, across a decade, is what turns ordinary incomes into something worth passing on.

Same market. Same interest rates. Same assets available to both couples. Completely different decade.

What keeps you going is something the best long-term investors understand intuitively - that wealth isn't something you accumulate for yourself. It's something you build for the people and the life that matter most to you.

Stewardship beats status. Every time. Every decade.

The couple who is building wealth because they want to prove something will make reactive decisions - buying at peaks, selling in panic, chasing whatever worked last year. The couple who is building wealth because they understand what it makes possible will make patient decisions. And in property and shares, patience is the single most powerful investment strategy available.

This is the first principle of the book. It isn't about tactics. It's about the reason behind everything that follows.

WEALTH BUILDERS THROUGH TIME

The Fuggers of Augsburg - Germany, 1480–1560

In the late 1400s, there was a textile merchant family from Augsburg, Germany: The Fuggers. This family was operating in one of the most unstable periods in European history; wars were frequent, and trade routes were shifting without warning. Political alliances were collapsing overnight. Entire merchant fortunes were wiped out not by bad decisions but by bad timing - being in the wrong place when the wrong king made the wrong move. The Fugger family had no guarantees. What they had was a philosophy.

Their conviction was simple, and it separated them from almost every contemporary: wealth must first create stability; only then can it safely pursue growth. They watched other families chase expansion without foundation and collapse under the first serious pressure. The Fuggers decided they would not make the same mistake.

They chose deliberate diversification at a time when most merchants concentrated everything in their primary trade. The Fuggers invested in productive land and then, significantly, in silver and copper mines across Central Europe. Physical assets that generated steady, predictable income regardless of what happened in the markets or the courts. Alongside those grounding assets, they expanded aggressively into banking, long-distance trade, and eventually the financing of monarchs and empires. They didn't choose between stability and growth. They built both simultaneously, each one protecting and enabling the other.

Other families thought the Fuggers were being cautious to the point of timidity. Why hold productive land when you could deploy that capital into high-margin trade? Why diversify when concentration is how fortunes are made quickly? The Fuggers held their position.

The result was one of the largest private fortunes in European history - and more importantly, one that endured. Their wealth survived wars, regime changes, and economic upheaval across generations. Not because they predicted the future. Because their structure could withstand almost any version of it.

The Fugger family were not building wealth for status or to win a competition with rival merchant families. They were building it as an act of stewardship - for their family, across time, against uncertainty. That clarity of purpose changed every decision they made.

The tools have changed. The principle hasn't.

An Australian couple in 2026 faces a different world - a mortgage instead of Central European silver mines, an ASX brokerage account instead of a banking empire- but the structural insight is identical: Stability first. Growth built on top of it. The reason for building in this way sits above status, above comparison and above what the neighbours are doing.

A PRESENT-DAY STORY

The Couple Who Found Their Why

Amy was a speech pathologist working three days a week at a community health centre in Glenelg. Will, her partner, was a logistics coordinator at a freight company in Outer Harbour. Between them they earned around $155,000 a year - not a lot by Sydney standards, but a real income in Adelaide, in a city where a decent house could still be bought without a decade of sacrifice. They owned their home in Seaton. They had a six-month-old daughter who slept in the room at the end of the hall. They had $11,000 in a savings account and no clear plan for what to do with it.

When asked why they wanted to build wealth, both of them gave the same answer without hesitating. "*Security*". That was the word. Security for their daughter. Security if one of them lost their job. Security so they could stop lying awake doing the same mental arithmetic that never quite balanced. It was an honest answer. And it was also the thing that had been quietly limiting them.

Beneath the answer sat an older belief that Amy had never quite examined. She had watched her father lose money on a managed fund in the early 2000s and concluded, reasonably, that investing was a game for people who understood things she didn't. She associated shares with risk, and property with safety, and she assumed in order to actually be useful – both those options required more money than they had. Will's belief was different but led to the same place. He thought they needed to earn more before they could start. "We'll invest when there's enough left over," he had said, more than once. *There was never enough left over.* There never is, for the couple who waits for surplus to appear on its own.

The conversation that changed things wasn't about products. It wasn't about tax structures or interest rates or the right suburb to buy in. It was a single question: "What does security actually look like for your family - not the feeling of it, but the real thing?" Amy answered first. She wanted to know that if Will's hours were cut - which had happened once already - they wouldn't need to sell anything. She wanted their daughter's school years to be free of the background hum of money anxiety. She wanted a rental property that paid its own way by the time their daughter started high school. Will's version was almost identical, word for word. Once the why was that clear, the decisions became easier. Not simple. Easier. They moved $9,000 of their savings into an offset account, which immediately began reducing their mortgage interest. They set up a joint brokerage account. And then? Then came the Tuesday night that Amy still talks about.

Their daughter was asleep. Will was in the lounge with the TV on, half-watching something neither of them would remember in a week. Amy sat at the kitchen table alone with her laptop. The plan, agreed on the week before, was $400 a month into a low-cost diversified ETF. Tonight she would choose the fund. She thought she would feel out of her depth. She did. She opened the brokerage account, navigated to the broad-market funds, read the descriptions of three of them, and picked one. It took twenty minutes. She closed the laptop and sat for a moment in the quiet. She thought she'd picked the wrong one. She picked it anyway. That was the part that mattered. Not the fund - the fund was fine. The act of choosing. She was no longer someone who didn't invest. She was someone who did.

Three years later, Amy and Will bought a unit in Woodville - a two-bedroom place that rented for $380 a week and was cash flow neutral from the first month. Their ETF portfolio had grown in the background, quietly, the way compounding works when you leave it alone. Their super balances were now something they actually checked. Their daughter was three and a half. The money anxiety hadn't disappeared entirely, but it had changed texture - from shapeless dread to something with edges they could see and work with.

The $400 a month wasn't the thing that changed their lives. The Tuesday night was. The moment they stopped being people who were planning to build wealth and became people who were doing it. The *why* - a daughter asleep down the hall, a mortgage that felt manageable, a retirement that wasn't a question mark - those were the things that made the life-changing Tuesday night possible. And that same why is what will keep them building long after the novelty has faded.

THE FOUNDATIONS OF THIS BOOK

This book has a simple argument, and it makes it across 13 chapters:

Property and shares, held together with discipline over time, are the most reliable wealth-building system available to an ordinary Australian couple.

Not the most exciting system. Not the fastest. *The most reliable.*

You don't need to be a financial genius. You don't need a six-figure investment portfolio before you start. You need two incomes (but this can work on one income as well, just a lot easier with two incomes), a long enough time horizon, and a reason to keep going when the market falls or the rate cycle turns.

The Australian tax system - through negative gearing, the capital gains discount, franking credits, and superannuation - is genuinely structured to reward the patient, long-term investor. Most dual-income couples pay significant tax their whole working lives without ever understanding that the system was designed to give some of it back to people who do exactly what this book describes.

Your combined income is not just your living standard. It is your primary wealth-building engine. Two incomes mean two super accounts, two concessional caps, two borrowing capacities working together. Most couples treat it as one income with a bonus. This book shows you what happens when you treat it as a system.

Each chapter will take one piece of that system - property cycles, share investing, debt management, tax strategy, the 14-year blueprint - and make it tangibly useful, not through charts and projections, but through real stories of people who have actually done it.

Some of those stories are historical. Most of them will be from ordinary Australian couples who made one or two structural decisions that changed the trajectory of their financial lives.

The decisions themselves are rarely dramatic. The outcomes, over a decade, usually are.

The Most Expensive Mistake Australian Couples Make

It isn't buying the wrong property. It isn't picking the wrong shares. It isn't even paying too much tax - though most dual-income couples do.

The most expensive mistake is *waiting.*

Waiting until the market is less uncertain. Waiting until the kids are older. Waiting until they understand it better. Waiting until they feel ready.

The couple who waits five years to start investing - not because they lacked the income, but because they lacked the clarity - doesn't lose five years. They lose the compounding of their money over five years. In property and shares, that gap is rarely recovered.

This book is designed to give you the clarity that removes the waiting. Not by overwhelming you with information. By giving you a framework simple enough to act on and true enough to trust.

You don't need more income to start building wealth. You need a clearer reason.

WEALTH BUILDER REFLECTION

One question to sit with:
If money stopped being a source of anxiety for your household, what would you spend your energy on instead - and what would it take to get there?

One truth to keep:
Wealth built from purpose outlasts wealth built from fear. The reason behind the plan is the plan.

Scan to download your free Couples Wealth Audit - know exactly where you stand before you build.

Chapter 1 begins with the question that most Australian couples never think to ask: why do you need both property and shares? And why does the answer matter more than almost anything else you'll decide as a couple?

PART ONE

The Wealth Builder Mindset

CHAPTER 1

Why You Need Both

The system that turns two ordinary assets into something extraordinary

It is a Sunday evening in Pymble, and Brendan and Kirra are sitting at the kitchen table with a laptop open between them. It's 2019.

They have been here before. The numbers spread across the screen - a mortgage, a savings account that never seems to grow fast enough - but tonight feels different. Tonight they made a decision. They are going to buy an investment property.

Brendan is a civil engineer. Kirra works in hospital administration. Together they earn around $275,000. They are not wealthy, but they are disciplined, and they have been watching the property market for eighteen months, waiting for the right moment.

'We should just do it,' Brendan says. 'Property always goes up. Everyone we know has done well out of it.'

Kirra nods. She trusts this. Her parents built their retirement on two investment properties. Her sister refinanced last year and bought a beach house. Property is the language her family speaks when they talk about getting ahead.

What neither of them says out loud - because they haven't thought to say it - is that they have never once talked about shares. Not seriously. Not as part of a plan. The ASX feels like something for people who know what they're doing; people who can afford to lose money... for people who are not them.

They close the laptop that night with the quiet confidence of people who have made up their minds.

Three years later, sitting at the same table, the mood is different.

The property has grown in value. That part worked exactly as they expected - the investment is sitting at roughly $180,000 more than they paid for it. On paper, they have built something real.

But in late 2022 the mortgage repayments climbed by nearly $1,100 a month. The cash flow that had felt comfortable tightened almost overnight. The surplus they had been quietly proud of - the buffer that was supposed to become a deposit on the next property - disappeared faster than either of them expected.

And then the moment came. A colleague mentioned it in passing: a two-bedroom unit two suburbs over, priced $60,000 below where it would have sat six months earlier. The vendor needed to move quickly. The opportunity was real.

Brendan rang the broker the next morning. They had the equity - the growth in the investment property was right there on the screen. But the bank wouldn't touch it. Borrowing capacity had been stretched by the first purchase and then compressed further by the rate rises. The equity existed. It just couldn't be unlocked. Not without income servicing that they no longer had room for.

They thought about selling. But they'd held the property for less than three years. Capital gains tax would take a significant slice of that $180,000 - and what was the point of selling an asset that was doing exactly what it was supposed to do, just to hand a portion of the gain to the ATO and end up with less than they started with?

The unit sold in a fortnight to someone else.

Kirra is staring at the screen now. The equity is right there. The opportunity is gone.

'We have wealth,' she says quietly. 'But we can't do anything with it.'

She's right. They built one engine, ran it hard, and found themselves trapped by their own success - too much equity to feel poor, not enough flexibility to move. The property did its job. The problem was that nothing else was running alongside it.

Two incomes don't equal twice the spending power. Two incomes mean five times the building power - but only if you build with both engines running.

The Myth

Property is not the enemy in this story. Property is part of the answer. But Brendan and Kirra - like most Australian couples - made an invisible assumption: that one asset class, chosen well and held long enough, would carry them where they wanted to go.

This chapter is about why that assumption is incomplete. Not wrong - *incomplete.* And why the difference between a good outcome and a great one is often not which asset you chose, but whether you ran both engines together.

It is also about a structural advantage that most Australian couples have, and almost none of them utilise fully: two incomes, two borrowing histories, two separate streams of income that can be pointed at more than one thing at once - a combined financial position that is genuinely more powerful than the sum of its parts. Not because of luck or brilliance, but because of how the system is designed to reward exactly this kind of partnership.

WEALTH BUILDERS THROUGH TIME

The Riddle of the Pastoral Dynasties - Colonial Australia, 1860–1920

We acknowledge the Aboriginal and Torres Strait Islander peoples as the traditional custodians of the land on which this story - and this country's wealth - was built.

In the decades after federation, two kinds of pastoral families shaped the Australian interior. Both started with land. Both worked extraordinarily hard. Both endured drought, flood, commodity shocks, and the long isolation of the outback. But sixty years later, their outcomes were almost unrecognisable from one another.

The first kind - the families historians remember - built empires that survived into the twentieth century and beyond: the Kidmans, the Tyson stations, the great western runs that stretched across three states. The second kind - far more numerous - were absorbed, sold up, or simply vanished from the records.

The difference between them had almost nothing to do with the quality of the land.

The families who endured held a belief the others didn't: that land alone, no matter how much of it you held, was one good drought away from ruin. They had watched their neighbours find this out the hard way. So they organised their affairs around a principle that was almost never spoken aloud but was visible in every decision they made.

They needed a second engine.

For most of the great pastoral dynasties, that second engine was wool processing, meatworks, or - increasingly from the 1880s onwards - bank shares and investment trusts. Some bought into the Bank of New South Wales. Others took positions in pastoral finance companies. A handful had relatives who understood the emerging share markets of Melbourne and Sydney and quietly directed family capital there.

The land produced income. The shares produced compounding.

The land anchored the family to Australia and to itself. The shares gave the family liquidity when drought years came - and the ability to buy more land when their less-prepared neighbours were forced to sell.

This was not a comfortable arrangement. In station culture, you were a grazier, or you weren't. Money in shares felt vaguely urban, vaguely soft, vaguely disloyal to the land that defined who you were. Some families resisted for a generation before necessity shifted their thinking. The ones who resisted longest are the ones who disappeared.

The ones who moved soonest - who decided that their loyalty was to the family, not to a single asset - are the ones who are still there.

By the early twentieth century, the dual-engine families had survived the Federation drought, the falls in wool prices, and two cycles of land devaluation that destroyed single-asset holdings across Queensland and New South Wales. Their share portfolios provided the liquidity to keep the stations running when income dried up. And when the market eventually rewarded patience - as it always does - the compounding in those share accounts quietly became as significant as the land itself.

What the great pastoral families understood - sometimes by design, sometimes only by surviving long enough to learn it - was that resilience is not the property of a single great asset. Resilience is what happens when two engines cover each other's weaknesses.

Land is illiquid. Shares are liquid. Land compounds slowly. Shares compound fast. Land requires patience. Shares require courage. When you hold both, the strengths overlap, and the weaknesses disappear.

The tools have changed. The principle hasn't.

PRESENT-DAY STORY

The Couple Who Built the Engine They Were Missing

James and Priya were not the kind of clients who came in a crisis. They came because they were doing well and had a feeling - accurate, as it turned out - that they were leaving something on the table. Combined income around $275,000. A home in Footscray they'd bought six years earlier and watched double. One investment property in Geelong, performing solidly. No shares. No second engine.

On paper, they were wealth builders. In practice, they were running one engine.

James was a committed property person. He had grown up watching his parents renovate and sell in Melbourne's outer suburbs, turning modest purchases into comfortable retirement. Property was real. Property made sense. Shares, to James, felt like a different game - one where he didn't know the rules and wasn't sure he wanted to learn them.

Priya was less fixed in her views but had always deferred to James on financial decisions. She wasn't against shares in principle. She had just never had a reason to think about them seriously.

What shifted things was a projection. Simple inputs - their current income, their existing equity, a modest monthly amount redirected into a broad index ETF alongside the property they were already holding. Not instead of property. *Alongside it.*

The fourteen-year numbers were not incrementally better. They were dramatically better. Not because shares are magic, but rather because the two engines together solved problems that each one alone couldn't. The property provided leverage and stability. The shares provided liquidity and compounding. The gap between the two scenarios - one engine versus two -

was not a rounding error. It was the difference between being trapped by their own equity and having genuine choices.

James stared at the projection for a long time as we sat in my office. Then he said something I hear often: 'Why didn't anyone show us this before?'

The early months were psychologically uncomfortable for James. He had spent years watching property and understanding exactly what price movements meant. Shares moved differently - faster, louder, without the satisfying solidity of a building he could drive past. When the market dipped 9 per cent in a bad quarter, he rang me.

I reminded him that his Geelong property had also quietly lost value in one of those years. He just hadn't seen the number in his banking app every morning.

Visibility is not volatility. What you can see doesn't define what's actually moving.

Three years after they started building both engines, James and Priya had something they hadn't had before: options. Not just wealth on paper - actual choices. When Priya's mother needed help with medical costs, they could move money without selling anything. When a development opportunity came up near their Geelong property, they had the liquidity to act quickly. When James was offered a role interstate that paid less but excited him far more, they could genuinely discuss it - not as a financial impossibility, but as a real decision.

Priya said it best: "We used to be asset rich. Now we feel like wealth builders. It's different."

James and Priya didn't change their income. They didn't take greater risks. They added a second engine - and the system they had been slowly building became genuinely resilient for the first time.

THE AUSTRALIAN APPLICATION
The Structural Edge Most Couples Are Sitting On

Here is the structural truth that most Australian couples don't see, even when they're looking right at it.

Two incomes, combined, don't just mean more money to spend. They mean a fundamentally different borrowing position, a fundamentally different tax profile, and a fundamentally different compounding machine - if the couple builds intentionally.

When banks assess a couple's borrowing capacity, they don't add two individual capacities together. They assess the combined household income against combined expenses and arrive at a number that is typically far higher than either person could access alone. This is not a trick. It is how the system is designed. It reflects the reality that two incomes provide a structural buffer that a single income simply cannot.

Most couples use this combined borrowing power to buy a home, and then stop. They treat the advantage as a one-time event - something that got them into the property - rather than as an ongoing engine.

But that combined borrowing power doesn't disappear once the home is purchased. It can be used again. And again. It can fund an investment property while maintaining share investments. It can support both a long-term property strategy and a regular ETF contribution program simultaneously, because two incomes mean two separate streams available for deployment.

The couple that treats their combined financial position as a system - not as two individual plans loosely coordinated - almost always outperforms the couple that doesn't. Not because they earned more. Because they built more deliberately with what they already had.

This is the structural edge that sits quietly inside every Australian dual-income household. The question is only whether they choose to use it.

Two incomes doesn't mean twice the spending power. It means five times the building power.

Why Property Alone Is Not Enough - And Why Shares Alone Isn't Either

Property does things shares cannot. It gives you leverage that banks will comfortably provide - 80 to 90 per cent in many cases - because the asset is stable, tangible, and relatively slow to move. It forces a discipline that shares don't: when you have a mortgage, you pay it. There is no choice. That enforced patience is genuinely valuable, especially in the early years of building wealth when the temptation to spend what you have is strongest.

Property also grows in a way that feels manageable to most people, because you can't see the price every morning. The homeowner who bought in Marrickville in 2012 didn't check the market value weekly. They just lived there, paid the mortgage, and watched the equity build quietly over a decade. That invisibility is a feature, not a bug. It removes the emotional noise that destroys returns in more liquid assets.

But property has limits that are genuinely structural, not just inconvenient.

You cannot sell 10 per cent of your investment property when you need liquidity. You cannot rebalance it without refinancing. When markets turn and opportunities emerge - as they do, reliably, every few years - property owners cannot move quickly enough to take advantage. Brendan and Kirra in Pymble experienced exactly this - equity sitting right there on the screen, a real opportunity two suburbs over, and no capacity to act. By the time they could have refinanced, the moment had passed.

Shares give you what property can't. *Liquidity* - the ability to act inside a week, sometimes inside a day. Scale - you can start with $500 and add $200 a fortnight. Global diversification - your investment is not tied to a single suburb, a single city, a single economy. And true compounding - dividends reinvested automatically, growing on themselves, without maintenance costs or tenant calls or strata fees.

Shares are also harder to hold. Their volatility is visible in a way property isn't. When the market drops 15 per cent in a month, you see it. When your property dips in value, you usually don't - and even if you did, you couldn't sell it in a panic. That forced illiquidity is property's gift to the impatient. Shares require the same patience, but they don't enforce it. You have to bring that yourself.

This is why both engines exist: Property instils discipline. Shares reward it.

What the System Actually Solves

When you run both engines – property and shares – together, you are not just diversifying. You are solving four problems that every household faces but rarely names.

1. Stability: something that holds its value through cycles and doesn't tempt you into panicked decisions. Property solves this. Its illiquidity, so often counted as a weakness, is the very thing that protects most investors from themselves.
2. Growth: something that compounds at a rate that actually changes your trajectory over ten and twenty years. Shares solve this. Broad index funds tracking the Australian and global markets have historically delivered returns that property, even leveraged property, has struggled to match over long periods.
3. Liquidity: actual access to money when life requires it. A job change. An opportunity. A family emergency. A business idea. Shares solve this too. They can be converted to cash in days. A property cannot.

4. Optionality - the feeling that you have choices, not just assets. This is the quiet benefit that Priya described when she said they used to be asset rich and now they felt like wealth builders. Optionality is not measured on a spreadsheet, but it is felt in every decision you make about work, family, and life. The household that has both engines running does not feel trapped by its own wealth.

One asset class, however good, solves two of these problems at best. The system solves all four.

The First Real Decision

Brendan and Kirra eventually sat down with a financial planner who asked them the same questions I asked. She showed them what their combined borrowing power looked like when they pointed it at both an investment property and a regular share investment simultaneously - running both engines together, from the same income, without waiting until one was finished before starting the other.

The numbers were not dramatic. Nothing about good wealth building ever is. But the direction was clear.

They didn't abandon the property plan. They kept it. But they added the second engine alongside it - a regular automated investment of 3 per cent of disposable income into a diversified index ETF, small at first, growing as their mortgage repayments became more manageable. Two years on, they had something they didn't have before.

Options. That is what this system is designed to give you. Not a shortcut. Not a trick. Not a promise about market conditions or interest rates or timing. Just the quiet, accumulating advantage of running two engines instead of one - for long enough that the engines do what compounding always does: reward patience at a scale that surprises even the people who were patient.

The pastoral families of colonial Australia knew this. James and Priya, watching a share portfolio grow quietly alongside two solid properties, know it now.

You don't need to choose between property and shares.

You need both.

WEALTH BUILDER REFLECTION

One question to sit with:
Which engine have we been running - and what would it look like to quietly start the second one alongside it?

One truth to keep:
Wealth built on one engine breaks under pressure. Wealth built on two engines bends, adapts, and compounds - across every cycle, every decade, every generation.

CHAPTER 2

The Risk of One-Basket Investing

Optionality is power

They found the house on a Saturday morning in April 2012. It was a three-bedroom weatherboard in Moranbah, Central Queensland, and it was listed at $715,000.

That price would have been absurd in most parts of Australia. In Moranbah, at the peak of the mining boom, it was the market.

Dan was a diesel fitter earning $185,000 a year on a fly-in, fly-out roster. Lisa managed the front office of a medical centre in Mackay, pulling in another $72,000. Combined income: $257,000. They were thirty-four and thirty-one, with a toddler and a second child on the way.

They'd bought their home in Mackay six years earlier, when Dan was still an apprentice and the Bowen Basin was just starting to heat up. They'd paid it down hard once the FIFO money started flowing - about $85,000 left on a place now worth close to $400,000. Not bad for a couple still in their early thirties. Now they wanted to build wealth. And in their world, in their town, in every conversation they'd had with mates and family and the broker who'd financed their first home, building wealth meant one thing.

Property.

Not just any property. Mining town property. The kind that had doubled in three years and showed no signs of slowing. Dan's site supervisor had two investment properties in the Bowen Basin. His brother-in-law had just settled on a place in Dysart. Everyone was doing it. The money was obvious.

They talked it through the way they talked through most things - carefully, practically, across a couple of weekends - and arrived at the same conclusion. The rental yield looked strong. The demand wasn't slowing. The broker's numbers made it look like the rent would cover the mortgage with room to spare. And they had the equity in their Mackay home to make it work without stretching themselves too far.

They bought the Moranbah house six weeks later.

Eighteen months after that, the coal price collapsed. The fly-in, fly-out workforce contracted. Rental demand in Moranbah fell off a cliff. The house they'd bought for $715,000 was revalued at $290,000, and they couldn't find a tenant at any price.

Dan kept his job, but the overtime disappeared. Lisa's hours were cut. They were still earning good money by most standards, but every spare dollar was now being fed into a mortgage on a property that had lost more than half its value.

They couldn't sell without crystallising a catastrophic loss. They couldn't refinance because the loan-to-value ratio had inverted. They couldn't invest in anything else because there was nothing left over.

They were trapped. Not by bad luck. By concentration.

The biggest risk isn't choosing the wrong asset. It's having no choice when you need one most.

The Myth

Dan and Lisa's story is not unusual. The details change - the suburb, the asset, the cycle - but the shape of it repeats across every generation of Australian investors. A couple with good income puts everything into a single bet, not because they're reckless, but because that bet is the only one they know. It's the one their parents made. The one their friends are making. The one that feels safest precisely because everyone around them is doing it.

And for a while, it works. Concentration always looks brilliant on the way up.

This chapter is about what happens on the way down. Not to frighten you - but to reframe what risk actually means for a dual-income Australian couple. Because the risk most couples fixate on - the risk of losing money - is rarely the risk that actually hurts them. The risk that hurts them is losing options. The ability to act. The ability to pivot. The ability to take advantage of the next opportunity when it appears, rather than watching it pass because every dollar is already committed to a single position.

Optionality is not a financial concept. It is a life concept. And it is the thing that concentration quietly destroys.

WEALTH BUILDERS THROUGH TIME

Marvellous Melbourne and the Crash of 1893

We acknowledge the Aboriginal peoples - including the Wurundjeri and Bunurong peoples of the Kulin Nation - as the traditional custodians of the land on which this story, and this city's wealth, was built.

In the 1880s, Melbourne was the richest city in the world per capita. The gold rush had faded but left behind something arguably more powerful: capital, confidence, and the unshakeable belief that the city's growth was permanent.

Land prices in Melbourne's inner suburbs had risen so consistently for so long that speculation had become indistinguishable from prudence. Banks lent freely against property. Building societies multiplied. Ordinary families - not just speculators - poured their savings into land, often borrowing against one block to buy the next.

The city expanded outward with the confidence of a place that had never known a serious correction. New suburbs were subdivided on the assumption that buyers would always appear. And for the better part of a decade, they did.

The prevailing belief was breathtakingly simple: Melbourne land could only go up. The city was growing. Immigration was strong. Capital was flowing in from London. The land itself was the guarantee.

This belief was held not just by the reckless but by the cautious. Schoolteachers, clerks, small business owners - people who thought of themselves as careful - put everything they had into Melbourne property because it felt like the safest place to be. They watched their neighbours grow wealthy and concluded that the risk was not in buying but in failing to buy.

Only a few held shares. Only a few held cash reserves beyond what was needed for daily life. The entire wealth of most middle-class Melbourne was concentrated in a single asset, in a single city, in a single market.

The families who survived - and in some cases thrived through the crash - were the ones who had made a different structural decision before the crisis arrived.

A small number of Melbourne's wealthier families, many of them connected to pastoral wealth or the remnants of the gold era, held diversified positions. They owned property, certainly - but they also held interests in pastoral companies, bank shares, insurance firms, and in some cases international investments through London-connected brokerages.

They were often mocked for their caution. In a city where land values doubled in five years, holding bank shares paying steady dividends seemed quaint. Holding cash reserves seemed cowardly.

Until it didn't.

The pressure to concentrate was immense. Melbourne in the late 1880s was a city drunk on property. Social gatherings revolved around land purchases. Newspapers ran daily columns on subdivision auctions. The man who held a diversified portfolio was the man who was accused of lacking conviction, of not believing in Melbourne, of being too clever by half.

The tension was not financial. It was social. Diversification meant standing apart from the crowd at precisely the moment when the crowd felt most certain. It meant trusting a principle over a feeling - and doing it for years before the principle was validated.

In 1891, the boom began to unravel. Building societies failed first, then the land banks, then the commercial banks themselves. Between 1891 and 1893, Melbourne property prices fell by as much as 50 per cent. In the outer suburbs - the areas that had been subdivided most aggressively - values fell further and did not recover for a generation.

Families who had concentrated everything in land were devastated. Not because the land became worthless - it didn't - but because they could not hold it. Mortgages were called. Building societies collapsed. Forced sales at the worst possible moment turned paper losses into permanent ones.

The diversified families lost money too. Their property holdings fell alongside everyone else's. But their bank shares, their pastoral interests, their cash reserves gave them what concentration could not: the ability to wait. And in some cases, the ability to buy. When Melbourne land was being sold at a fraction of its pre-crash value, the families who had capital available acquired properties that would prove to be the foundation of multi-generational wealth.

Concentration had looked like confidence. In the end, it was fragility dressed as conviction.

The families who survived Marvellous Melbourne's crash did not predict it. They did not time it. They simply held a structure that could absorb it. Their diversification was not a bet against Melbourne. It was a bet on their own ability to endure whatever happened next.

The tools have changed. The principle hasn't.

A PRESENT-DAY STORY

The Couple Who Learned What Concentration Costs

Steph and Andrew came to see me in early 2019. Andrew was a project manager in construction earning around $155,000. Steph worked in HR for a mid-tier firm in Parramatta on about $85,000. Two kids under ten. A home in the Hills District they'd bought in 2011, and three investment properties - two in Western Sydney held in Andrew's name, one in Newcastle held jointly.

They'd built the portfolio progressively over seven years, each purchase funded by the equity created by the one before it. The two properties in Andrew's name - a house in Blacktown and a townhouse near Penrith - were negatively geared against his income, which made sense structurally. The Newcastle unit was in both names.

On paper, the portfolio looked strong. Combined property value around $2.4 million. Equity of roughly $750,000. They had done what every property-focused Australian dreams of doing: built a portfolio through discipline, leverage, and patience.

They had zero shares. No managed funds. Their superannuation sat in default options neither of them had examined in years.

Andrew's philosophy was clear and deeply held: property is real, property is safe, and property is how wealth is built in this country. He had watched his parents do it. He had done it himself. Every dollar of surplus income went toward the next deposit, the next purchase, the next rung on the property ladder.

Steph trusted the plan. She'd watched the equity build year after year and felt the same quiet pride Andrew did - they were ahead of most couples their age, and they'd done it themselves.

But Andrew had started to feel something he couldn't quite name. Despite the portfolio on paper, their month-to-month life felt tight. Three investment mortgages, insurance across four properties, property management fees, maintenance, council rates, land tax, strata on the Newcastle unit - the carrying costs were relentless. When one tenant left the Blacktown house, and it sat vacant for eleven weeks, the cash flow pressure was immediate and uncomfortable.

He didn't raise it with Steph directly - not at first. Raising it felt like doubting the plan he'd built. But he'd started doing the sums late at night after she'd gone to bed, trying to work out why $240,000 in combined income and nearly three-quarters of a million in equity still left them feeling stretched.

The shift came from a conversation about what they actually wanted.

Steph wanted to reduce her hours when the youngest started school - move to four days a week, maybe three. Andrew wanted the freedom to take a role that paid less but involved less travel. Both wanted to feel less dependent on every property performing perfectly every quarter.

When we mapped out their position honestly, the picture confirmed what Andrew had been sensing. Their property portfolio was strong but illiquid. Every dollar of equity was locked inside bricks and mortgage structures. If Steph reduced her income, their serviceability on the loans tightened. If Andrew changed roles, it tightened further. The portfolio that was supposed to create freedom had, paradoxically, reduced it.

The decision we made together was not dramatic. They didn't sell everything. They sold the Newcastle unit - the jointly held property with the lowest growth potential and the highest maintenance burden. After capital gains tax and costs, they netted approximately $165,000.

That capital went into three places. First, $60,000 into an offset account against their home loan, immediately reducing their interest payments and freeing up monthly cash flow. Second, $25,000 into Steph's super as a non-concessional contribution, starting to close the gap between their two balances. Third, $80,000 as the foundation of a diversified share portfolio - split between an Australian index ETF and a global index ETF.

The critical structural move was what happened next. With the Newcastle mortgage gone and the offset reducing interest on the home loan, their monthly carrying costs dropped by close to $3,000. That freed up enough room to set up a dollar cost averaging plan - $1,500 a month flowing automatically into the share portfolio on the same day each month, buying at whatever price the market offered. No timing. No decisions. Just the discipline of showing up regularly.

The two remaining investment properties stayed in Andrew's name, negatively geared against his higher income. That structure meant Steph's income wasn't propping up the carrying costs - which is what would eventually make it possible for her to reduce her hours without the whole system buckling. For the first time in their investing lives, they had two engines.

Andrew hated selling the Newcastle unit. He felt it physically. Every property he'd bought represented a win, a step forward, proof that the plan was working. Selling one felt like going backwards.

But the harder adjustment was subtler than grief over a sold property. It was the absence of something tangible. Andrew could drive past his Blacktown investment on the way home from a site visit and feel something - ownership, progress, solidity. The share portfolio existed only as a number on a screen. It didn't have a street address. It didn't have a tenant. He couldn't point to it and say: "I built that".

He found himself checking the share app six times a day. Green one morning, red the next. Steph noticed before he did. 'You never once checked what the Blacktown place was worth,' she told him one evening. 'But you've looked at that app three times since dinner.'

She was right. And the reason mattered. He watched the shares because they moved in front of him. The properties moved too, but slowly and silently, behind a wall of quarterly statements he rarely opened. The discomfort Andrew felt wasn't about risk. It was about attention. Shares demanded a kind of discipline property had never asked of him: the discipline to look away.

It took him about four months to learn it. By then, he'd stopped checking daily. Not because the numbers had improved, but because he'd finally understood that watching something closely and managing it well are not the same thing.

Then came March 2020. When COVID hit, and the ASX fell 35 per cent in five weeks, Andrew and Steph had something most property-concentrated couples did not: liquid capital. While property investors around them froze - unable to act, unable to buy, unable to do anything except wait and hope their tenants kept paying rent - Steph and Andrew kept their dollar cost averaging running.

They didn't increase it. They didn't panic-buy. They simply didn't stop. The $1,500 a month kept going in, buying more units at lower prices, exactly when the market was offering the best value it had presented in a decade.

Their jobs held. Construction slowed for the first few weeks of lockdown but surged once HomeBuilder and infrastructure spending kicked in - Andrew was busier than ever by mid-year. Steph's HR role became critical as her firm navigated stand-downs, JobKeeper applications, and return-to-work policies. Neither of them missed a pay cycle.

By mid-2021, the shares they'd purchased during the COVID period had grown more than 40 per cent. Their remaining two investment properties had also recovered and then some. Their offset account had continued reducing interest on their home loan. And because Andrew's negatively geared properties weren't drawing on Steph's income, she had dropped to four days a week - a decision that would have been financially impossible eighteen months earlier.

Andrew said something in our last meeting that I think about often: 'I used to think selling that property was a mistake. Now I think it was the best financial decision we ever made. Not because of the money. Because of the options.'

Steph and Andrew didn't get smarter. They didn't earn more. They didn't predict COVID or time the market. They simply exchanged a small amount of concentration for a significant amount of optionality. And when the world shifted in a way nobody foresaw, that optionality was worth more than the asset they'd sold to create it.

THE AUSTRALIAN APPLICATION

The Hidden Reward for Patience Across Both Assets

Here is something most Australian couples have heard of but very few have thought about strategically: the capital gains tax discount.

The rule is straightforward. If you hold an asset - a property, a parcel of shares, an ETF position - for longer than twelve months before selling, you pay capital gains tax on only half the gain. The other half is simply exempt. For a dual-income couple in the middle- to upper-tax brackets, this is not a minor concession. It is one of the most significant wealth-building incentives in the Australian tax system.

But here is what makes it genuinely powerful for the couple who holds both property and shares: the discount applies identically to both asset classes. It doesn't favour property over shares or shares over property. It rewards patience equally, regardless of where the gain was made.

This matters more than it first appears.

The couple who holds only property gets the CGT discount when they eventually sell an investment property - an event that might happen once or twice in a decade, involves substantial transaction costs, and often triggers a complex capital gains event that is difficult to manage strategically.

The couple who holds both property and shares has far more control over when and how they realise gains. They can choose which asset to sell, in which financial year, against which income. They can stagger the timing of gains across both partners. They can offset a capital gain in one asset against a capital loss in another. They can use the discount strategically, rather than just hopefully.

This is optionality expressed through the tax system. The diversified couple doesn't just have more assets. They have more levers. More choices. More ways to structure their wealth in a way that keeps more of it in their hands and less of it in the ATO's.

And because the discount rewards holding for twelve months or more, it structurally discourages the short-term thinking that destroys returns. It is, in effect, the tax system telling you what this book is telling you: hold patiently, hold broadly, and the law will reward you for it.

The couple who holds both assets doesn't just build more wealth. They keep more of it.

What Concentration Actually Costs

It is worth naming what concentration takes from you, because the cost is rarely visible until it's too late.

1. **Time**: Dan and Lisa spent three years managing the consequences of their Moranbah investment - three years of financial and emotional energy directed at damage control rather than wealth building. The opportunity cost of those years - the investments they didn't make, the compounding they missed, the strategies they couldn't pursue - will never be recovered.
2. **Stress:** A concentrated portfolio doesn't just carry financial risk. It carries emotional risk. When your entire wealth is in one asset, and that asset declines, the stress is not proportional - it is total. It affects sleep, relationships, decision-making, and the ability to think clearly about anything else. Andrew described the eleven-week vacancy on the Blacktown house as the period when he first started doing the sums late at night, alone, trying to understand why everything looked right on paper and felt wrong in practice. That is the emotional tax of concentration.
3. **Lost Optionality:** The third cost is the one that matters most for the reader of this book. The concentrated couple cannot take advantage of opportunities when they appear. They cannot reduce their working hours. They cannot change careers. They cannot say yes to the thing that would make their lives better, because every dollar is already committed and every decision is constrained by a single position.

Diversification is not a hedge against disaster. Most couples will never experience a Moranbah-level correction. Diversification is a hedge against rigidity - against the slow, quiet loss of choices that comes from building your entire financial life on one foundation, no matter how solid that foundation appears.

The Real Risk

Most Australians, when they think about investment risk, think about losing money. They picture a share price falling, a property market correcting. a balance going down instead of up.

That is one kind of risk. It is the kind that makes headlines and keeps people awake at night.

But it is not the kind that actually changes outcomes over a decade.

The risk that changes outcomes is structural. It is the risk of being unable to act. Unable to adapt. Unable to respond when life - which does not consult your portfolio before it shifts - demands a response.

A rate rise. A redundancy. A family illness. A once-in-a-decade buying opportunity. These are not hypotheticals. They are certainties. Not any one of them specifically, but the category: unexpected things will happen during the fourteen years you are building wealth. The question is whether your structure gives you the ability to respond, or whether it locks you in place and forces you to absorb the impact.

The couple who holds property and shares and super and an offset account - who has built their wealth across multiple engines rather than a single one - can respond. They have liquid capital. They have assets they can draw on without selling the ones they want to keep. They have choices.

The couple who has concentrated everything in a single asset, no matter how good that asset is, can only wait.

Risk is not what happens to your portfolio. Risk is what your portfolio prevents you from doing when life moves.

WEALTH BUILDER REFLECTION

One question to sit with:

If one of your assets lost half its value tomorrow, would the rest of your position give you the ability to wait - or would it force you to react?

One truth to keep:

Concentration feels like conviction. Diversification feels like compromise. But over a decade, couples with options always outperform - and live a happier life.

Chapter 3 asks the question that naturally follows: if property is one of your two engines, how do you choose the right property - and what do the couples who get it right actually do differently from the ones who don't?

PART TWO

Building Wealth with Property

CHAPTER 3

Picking the Right Property

Behaviour beats intelligence

They almost bought the wrong house.

It was a Wednesday evening in late October, and Danielle and Matt were driving back from an open inspection in Marsden Park. The listing had ticked every box on the spreadsheet Matt had been building for six months - four bedrooms, two bathrooms, a new build on a compact lot in a master-planned estate, listed at $780,000. The suburb had grown 9 per cent the previous year. A new shopping centre was coming. The median number of days on the market was sitting at just fourteen. Properties were moving fast, and the agent had made sure they knew it.

But Danielle hadn't said a word since they left.

'What's wrong?' Matt asked.

'I don't know. Something about it.'

Matt waited.

'It felt desperate,' she said. 'The agent. The vendor. The whole thing. Like everyone in that room needed us to buy it more than we needed to own it.'

Matt had felt it too. He just hadn't wanted to say it, because the spreadsheet said yes and they'd been looking for eight months and he was tired of looking.

They drove home in silence. That night, Matt did something he hadn't done before. He stopped looking at what the suburb had done and started looking at why. What he found changed the way they thought about property entirely.

The growth in Marsden Park had been driven almost exclusively by new land releases - not by the kind of organic, supply-constrained demand that sustains long-term value. Hundreds of near-identical homes were being built simultaneously across multiple estates, with more stages approved and more land earmarked for release. The shopping centre, when he read the planning documents properly, was still two years from completion and anchored by a single supermarket. The rental yield on comparable properties was sitting below 3 per cent, which meant the investment case depended entirely on continued capital growth - and the driver of that growth was already slowing as supply flooded in.

He checked the vendor discounting data. Properties that had been listed eight weeks earlier were now selling at 5 to 7 per cent below their original asking price. The fourteen-day median the agent had quoted was accurate - but only because the vendors who couldn't get their price had already pulled their listings. The properties that were selling fast were the ones that had already been discounted.

They didn't buy the Marsden Park property. Within twelve months, the suburb's median had softened further as hundreds of new completions hit the market simultaneously. The house they'd inspected was relisted eighteen months later at $710,000 - $70,000 below the price they'd almost paid.

Danielle's gut had been right. But what mattered more was what happened next: the conversation they had that night about what 'right' actually meant. Not what felt exciting. Not what the spreadsheet said in isolation. Not what the agent was selling. What would still be a good decision in fourteen years, regardless of what the market did tomorrow.

That conversation is what this chapter is about.

The best property decision most couples will ever make is not the one that looks smartest. It's the one they can hold through the worst year without flinching.

The Myth

Every Australian couple who sets out to buy an investment property faces the same invisible problem. They have too much information and not enough judgement.

They can find median prices, rental yields, vacancy rates, infrastructure plans, population projections, and auction clearance rates for any suburb in the country. They can read twelve articles on the best suburbs to invest in and get twelve different answers. They can model cash flow scenarios on three different calculators and still not know whether the property in front of them is the right one.

The information is not the problem. The problem is that most couples use information to confirm a decision they've already made emotionally - and then call that research.

This chapter is about what separates the couples who build lasting wealth through property from the ones who get lucky once and never quite understand why they can't replicate it. It is not a formula for picking the right suburb. Formulas age badly, and they encourage the exact kind of false confidence that put Dan and Lisa into Moranbah - a decision that Chapter 2 explored in detail, and that most Australian property investors recognise as the cautionary tale it is.

The difference, almost always, is not intelligence. It's behaviour.

WEALTH BUILDERS THROUGH TIME

The Immigrants Who Bought What Nobody Wanted - Sydney, 1950–1980

In the three decades following the Second World War, a wave of migration reshaped Sydney in ways that are still visible today. Greek, Italian, Lebanese, and later Vietnamese families arrived with almost nothing - limited English, limited capital, limited connections. What they had was a relationship with property that most Australian-born families of the era did not share.

For the established middle class of 1950s Sydney, the 'right' suburbs were the ones their parents had lived in. The North Shore. The Eastern Suburbs. Places where the schools were known, the streets were leafy, and the social infrastructure was already built. These suburbs were expensive, competitive, and emotionally loaded with status and belonging.

The migrant families could not afford those suburbs. So they went where the established families would not.

The belief that separated the migrant property buyers from their Australian-born contemporaries was not a sophisticated investment thesis. It was survival logic, forged in countries where property ownership was the single most important determinant of whether a family endured or disappeared. A house is not a lifestyle statement. It is a productive asset. You do not buy where you want to be seen. You buy where you can afford to buy - and then you hold it.

They did not read market reports. They read the land itself - the proximity to transport, the width of the block, the distance to employment, the direction the city was growing. And because they were buying on affordability rather than prestige, they ended up in suburbs where those fundamentals were quietly strong.

They bought in Marrickville, Leichhardt, Dulwich Hill, Canterbury, Lakemba, Bankstown. Suburbs that the North Shore and Eastern Suburbs families of the 1950s and 1960s considered working-class at best, undesirable at worst. The houses were modest. The streets were unfashionable. The entry prices were a fraction of what the established suburbs commanded.

To understand what that fraction meant in practice: in the early 1960s, before Australia switched to decimal currency in 1966, a modest weatherboard in Marrickville might have cost £4,000 to £5,500 (roughly $8,000 to $11,000 in decimal terms). A comparable home in Vaucluse or Rose Bay - the kind of harbourside suburb the established families aspired to - would have been three to five times that, £15,000 or more ($30,000 or higher). The migrant family who arrived with £5,000 in savings didn't have a choice about which suburb to enter. The market made the choice for them.

But here is what the market didn't decide: what those families did next. And what they did next is the part that matters most.

The family who bought in Marrickville in 1962 started building equity immediately. While the family who dreamed of Vaucluse spent three to five more years saving for a deposit they could afford, the Marrickville family was building equity, collecting rent if they'd moved on to a second property, and compounding their position year after year. At roughly 8 to 9 per cent compound annual growth - which is what inner Sydney property delivered over that period - every year of delay cost the Vaucluse saver dearly. You do not get those years back. The couple who enters the market three years earlier does not just have a three-year head start. They have three years of compounding that the late starter can never recover.

And the families who could only afford Marrickville had a second, less obvious advantage: they could accumulate. As each property grew in value, the equity it generated gave them the capacity to buy the next one. Not simultaneously - sequentially, over decades, through the combination of rising values and the willingness to live modestly in order to own broadly. A family might live in a small fibro house while renting out the larger brick home next door. The ego cost was zero, because the goal was never appearance. The goal was ownership.

By the time a family had accumulated three properties - even modest ones across different suburbs or, ideally, different cities - they had something the single-property owner in Vaucluse never had: structural optionality. Three assets meant three independent income streams, three different market exposures, and the ability to sell or restructure one position without dismantling the entire portfolio. If one market softened, the other two held. If one property needed to be sold to fund a child's first home or restructure debt, the family still had two assets working. A single property, no matter how prestigious, is a concentrated bet. *Three properties is a system.*

This is a distinction the book will return to in later chapters. For now, the principle is simple: even if you could afford the premium suburb, spreading the same capital across multiple properties in structurally sound, affordable markets creates more resilience, more optionality, and more ways to adapt as your life and your circumstances change.

None of this mattered to the migrant families for the reason most investors would expect. They were not building a portfolio to optimise returns. They were building security. The properties were not places they wanted to live - they were assets they wanted to own. That separation between the investment and the identity is the behavioural edge that most modern Australian couples have lost, and it is the single most important lesson in this chapter.

The tension these families faced was not financial. It was social. They were buying in suburbs that the dominant culture had explicitly rejected. They were making decisions that looked foolish to anyone who measured property success by postcode prestige rather than long-term fundamentals.

And they endured something harder than financial risk: they endured being right for a very long time before anyone noticed. A family who bought in Marrickville in 1962 for £5,200 (around $10,400) would not see that decision validated by the broader market for twenty years. For two decades, the North Shore families continued to believe they had made the smarter choice. The Marrickville family just kept holding, kept building equity, and kept buying the next one.

By the 1990s, the map had redrawn itself. The inner-west suburbs that the migrant families had bought into were now among the most desirable in Sydney. Marrickville, Leichhardt, Dulwich Hill, Petersham - suburbs that had been dismissed for decades were suddenly commanding prices that rivalled the established east.

Today, the median house price in Marrickville sits above $2.2 million. To put that in perspective: £5,200 in 1962 is equivalent to roughly $191,000 in today's money when you adjust purely for inflation. The property didn't deliver $191,000 of value. It delivered $2.2 million - roughly $2 million above what inflation alone would have produced. That is more than eleven times the inflation-adjusted value, from a single modest purchase that the buyer could barely afford at the time.

Did the premium suburbs do better? Marginally, yes. Vaucluse, which commanded £15,000 or more in the early 1960s, now carries a median house price above $9.5 million - roughly 9.5 per cent compound annual growth compared to Marrickville's 8.8 per cent. On a single property, the premium suburb outperformed by a fraction of a percentage point per year.

But the family who waited three to five years to save enough for Vaucluse missed three to five years of compounding at the lower entry point. And the family who bought three Marrickville properties sequentially over two decades - using the equity growth in each to fund the next - built a portfolio now worth $6 to $7 million across multiple assets, with the flexibility to sell one, restructure another, and hold the third. The Vaucluse family built one magnificent asset. The Marrickville family built a system.

Both families built generational wealth. But only one family built it in a way that could absorb a setback, adapt to a changing life, and be divided among the next generation without being destroyed in the process.

The migrant families of post-war Sydney did not outperform because they were smarter. They outperformed because they were less distracted. They had no attachment to postcode prestige. No social pressure to buy in the 'right' suburb. No emotional need for the property to impress anyone. They never confused the investment with the lifestyle. They bought what they could afford, they started immediately, they accumulated patiently, and they held long enough for the fundamentals to be proven right.

Behaviour beat intelligence. Patience beat analysis. And the willingness to be unfashionable for twenty years built more wealth than all the clever timing in the world.

The tools have changed. The principle hasn't.

A PRESENT-DAY STORY

The Couple Who Stopped Looking for Perfect

Adam and Emily had been searching for their first investment property for fourteen months when they came to see me. Adam was an electrical engineer. Emily taught Year 4 at a public school in Adelaide's eastern suburbs. Combined income around $195,000. They owned their home in Mitcham with roughly $310,000 in total equity - of which about $180,000 was usable, meaning the amount they could access while keeping their home loan at or below 80 per cent of the property's value. Their borrowing capacity was solid. Their savings discipline was genuinely impressive - they had $62,000 in an offset account they'd built over three years of consistent effort.

They were ready. They had been ready for over a year. And they still hadn't bought.

The problem was not the market. The problem was the process they'd built around the decision. Adam had constructed an elaborate scoring system - a spreadsheet with fourteen weighted criteria covering everything from population growth to school catchment quality to infrastructure pipeline proximity. Every property they inspected was scored against the matrix. Every Saturday was spent at open inspections. Every Sunday was spent updating the spreadsheet.

In fourteen months, they had inspected over sixty properties. Adam's spreadsheet had scored eleven of them above his threshold. Of those eleven, Emily had liked seven. Of those seven, four had sold before they made an offer. The three they did bid on, they were outbid each time - because by the time the spreadsheet had confirmed the decision, someone less analytical had already moved.

Adam believed - sincerely and completely - that the right property could be identified through rigorous analysis. That if he built a good enough model, the answer would reveal itself. That the couples who got property investing wrong were the ones who hadn't done enough research.

He was half right. Couples who do no research make avoidable mistakes. But Adam had crossed the line that separates useful research from expensive procrastination. His spreadsheet had become a mechanism for avoiding the one thing research cannot provide: the willingness to act with incomplete information.

Because every property decision is made with incomplete information. Every single one. The couple who waits for certainty is the couple who watches the market move without them.

The conversation that changed things was not about spreadsheets. It was about what the spreadsheet was actually protecting Adam from.

I asked him a question: 'What happens if you buy a property and it doesn't perform the way you expect in the first two years?'

He paused. 'That's what I'm trying to avoid.'

'I know. But what actually happens? Walk me through it.'

When he did, the fear became specific and manageable. A property that underperforms for two years, purchased at a sensible price with a solid tenant, is not a catastrophe. It is a holding pattern. The mortgage gets paid. The tax benefit flows. The equity builds slowly instead of quickly. It is uncomfortable, not devastating.

What was actually devastating - and what Adam had not modelled - was the cost of the fourteen months he'd already spent not buying—the compounding he'd missed. The equity growth in the properties he'd scored highly and then watched someone else buy. The rent he could have been collecting. The tax deductions he could have been claiming.

The spreadsheet had been protecting him from a moderate downside while guaranteeing a significant one.

We simplified the criteria to five things that actually matter over a decade: established suburb with fixed land supply, proximity to employment and transport, rental demand strong enough to find a tenant within three weeks, a purchase price they could service comfortably if rates rose two percentage points, and a property they wouldn't need to sell for at least ten years.

Six weeks later, they bought a solid three-bedroom house in Elizabeth Park, north of Adelaide. It wasn't exciting. It didn't score highest on the old spreadsheet. But it met every one of the five criteria, and they could hold it through anything the market threw at them.

Adam struggled with the purchase for the first six months. He kept running the numbers. He kept comparing the Elizabeth Park property to the ones he'd let slip during the fourteen months of searching. A house in Prospect that had grown 11 per cent since they'd scored it. A unit in Unley that had been rezoned and jumped in value.

Emily saw it differently. She saw a tenanted property generating $420 a week in rent, a mortgage that was comfortable even after the latest rate rise, and a tax return that had shifted meaningfully in their favour for the first time. She saw something they hadn't had fourteen months ago: momentum.

'We're building now,' she said one evening. 'We weren't building before. We were just researching.'

That landed harder than any spreadsheet ever had.

Two years after the Elizabeth Park purchase, Adam and Emily's position had shifted in ways the spreadsheet would never have predicted. The property had grown modestly - around 5 per cent per year, nothing spectacular. But the rental income had been consistent, the negative gearing benefit had reduced their annual tax bill meaningfully, and - most importantly - the discipline of owning and managing an investment had changed the way they made financial decisions together.

They had started a small share investment alongside the property. They had consolidated their super funds and switched to a growth allocation. They had begun thinking like wealth builders rather than property shoppers.

The Elizabeth Park house was not their best investment. It was their first investment. And the difference between the couple who owns a solid first investment and the couple who is still searching for a perfect one is not measured in returns. It is measured in years.

Adam and Emily didn't find a better property, but they became better buyers. They stopped letting the pursuit of the optimal prevent the achievement of the excellent. They traded fourteen criteria for five, certainty for confidence, and a perfect spreadsheet for an imperfect but real asset that started compounding the moment they signed.

The property didn't need to be the best decision they ever made. It needed to be a decision they could hold for a decade without stress. That is a fundamentally different filter - and it is the one that separates the couples who build wealth from the ones who study it.

THE AUSTRALIAN APPLICATION

The Hidden Subsidy for Getting Started

Here is something that Adam's spreadsheet never captured, and it is arguably the most powerful reason to stop searching and start owning: the Australian tax system has, for decades, paid investors to hold property. Not figuratively. Literally.

Negative gearing is the mechanism, and most Australian couples have heard of it without ever understanding what it actually does for them personally. So let's simplify it.

When you own an investment property, the costs of holding that property - mortgage interest, council rates, insurance, property management fees, depreciation, maintenance - are tax-deductible against your income. If those costs exceed the rental income the property generates, the difference is a tax loss. And historically, that loss has reduced the amount of income tax you pay from your regular job.

For a dual-income couple in the middle tax brackets, this has not been a minor benefit. It has been a structural subsidy that materially transforms the economics of holding an investment property - particularly in the early years when the mortgage interest is highest, and the gap between costs and rental income is widest.

One component that most couples dramatically undervalue is *depreciation.* Unlike interest and rates, depreciation is a non-cash deduction. You don't actually spend the money - but you claim it as if you did. The building itself, the carpets, the blinds, the hot water system, the kitchen appliances - all of these can be depreciated over time, and for a relatively new property the depreciation schedule can add $8,000 to $15,000 a year in deductions. That is often the single largest contributor to the paper loss that drives the tax benefit, and it costs the investor nothing out of pocket. It is, in practical terms, a deduction for owning the property - and it is the piece most of my clients overlook entirely.

Take Adam and Emily's Elizabeth Park property as a practical example. The rental income covered most of the mortgage repayment. But once you added the interest component, the council rates, the insurance, the management fees, and - critically - the depreciation on the building and fittings, the property ran at a loss on paper of roughly $12,000 a year. That loss was split between Adam and Emily's individual tax returns, reducing each of their taxable incomes by $6,000.

For Adam, earning around $115,000, that $6,000 reduction saved him approximately $2,280 in tax. For Emily, earning around $80,000, it saved her approximately $1,950. Combined: over $4,200 returned to them by the ATO in the first year alone and not as a one-off benefit, but as an annual structural advantage that persisted for as long as they held the property and the costs exceeded the income.

The part that most couples miss? That tax saving wasn't reducing their wealth. It was subsidising the holding cost of an asset that was simultaneously building equity and growing in value. The government was effectively paying them to become wealthier - provided they had the patience to hold.

What Is Changing in Governance - And What Isn't

A note on timing. In the May 2026 Federal Budget, the government proposed significant changes to negative gearing for residential property, effective from 1 July 2027. These changes had not yet passed the Senate at the time of writing, but the direction is clear and worth understanding now.

Under the proposed changes, negative gearing in its current form - where rental losses offset your salary and other income - will be limited to new build properties only. If you purchase an established residential property after budget night (12 May 2026) and hold it past 1 July 2027, the rental losses will be quarantined. That means you can still claim them, but only against other residential property income or capital gains from residential property - not against your salary or wages.

If you already own an investment property, nothing changes. Properties held before budget night are grandfathered under the existing rules. And if you buy a new build - a property that genuinely adds to housing supply, such as a dwelling built on vacant land or a site where an existing home is demolished and replaced with a greater number of dwellings - the full negative gearing benefit remains intact, along with the existing 50 per cent CGT discount or a choice to use the new index method system.

This is a deliberate policy shift: the government is directing investor activity toward new housing supply. For the couples reading this book, it means the decision between an established property and a new build now carries a different tax consequence than it did before. The incentive to buy new is real and meaningful.

But the underlying principle of this chapter has not changed. Whether you buy established or new, the question remains the same: *can you hold this property for a decade through a rate rise, a vacancy, and a flat year?* A new build in a supply-flooded estate that you cannot hold is still a worse decision than an established property in a constrained suburb that you can - even if the tax treatment is less generous.

The tax incentive changes the calculus. It does not change the discipline. The couple who buys for holdability, who buys within their budget with a margin of safety, and who holds with patience will still outperform the couple who chases the best tax outcome into a property they cannot sustain.

The tax system doesn't reward the cleverest property investor. It rewards the most patient one.

What the Right Property Actually Looks Like

Here is what the couples who get property right *actually* do - not as a formula, but as a pattern of behaviour that shows up again and again across decades.

They buy in established suburbs. Not new developments. Not fringe releases. Not the next big thing. Established suburbs with existing infrastructure, existing demand, and - critically - a fixed supply of land. When a suburb can be replicated by building another one next to it, the scarcity premium disappears. When the land is finite, and the demand is structural, time works in your favour. The new build tax incentives discussed above may shift this preference for some couples, and that's a conversation worth having with your adviser - but the principle of supply constraint still governs long-term value regardless of the tax treatment.

They buy what tenants want, not what they would want to live in themselves. This is the behavioural trap that catches more first-time property investors than any market downturn. You walk through the house imagining yourself living there - the kitchen, the bathroom, the garden - rather than imagining the tenant who will pay you rent for the next ten years. The tenant wants proximity to work, functional rooms, and reliable transport. The tenant does not care about the splashback tiles.

They buy at a price that fits within their budget - with room to spare. Not the maximum the bank will lend them. Not the price that works perfectly at today's interest rates. The price they can still service if rates go up two points, if one of them loses their income for six months, or if the property sits vacant for two months between tenants. The buffer is not optional. The buffer is the strategy.

They buy boring properties. The couples who build lasting property wealth almost never buy the exciting one. They buy the solid brick three-bedroom in the established suburb with the reliable school and the bus route to the CBD. They buy it, they rent it, and they hold it for a decade while everyone around them chases something more glamorous. The boring property doesn't make for a good dinner party story. It makes for a good wealth-building engine.

And they stop looking once they've bought. This is the behaviour that separates wealth builders from property enthusiasts. The wealth builder buys, holds, and redirects their energy toward the next piece of the system - shares, super, debt management, the second property when the time is right. The property enthusiast buys, then spends the next three years checking comparable sales and wondering if they should have waited. One of these behaviours compounds. The other corrodes.

The Research That Changes Property Decisions

Remember what Matt did the night he and Danielle drove home from that Marsden Park inspection? He stopped looking at what the suburb had done and started looking at *why*. That shift - from surface data to structural understanding - is the difference between research that confirms a feeling and research that changes a decision.

Most couples research property the way they shop for a car: they start with what they want and then look for evidence that it's a good choice. The couples who build lasting wealth do it the other way around. They start wide, understand the structure, and let the research narrow the field until the right property reveals itself. Not the perfect property. The holdable one.

That research moves through five layers, from the broadest to the most specific. No single layer gives you the answer. But together, they give you something more valuable than certainty: confidence that the decision is structurally sound.

The city and the region come first

The question at this level is not 'which city is growing fastest?' It's 'which city has a diversified economy that doesn't depend on a single industry?' Moranbah - where Dan and Lisa bought at the peak of the mining boom and watched their property lose more than half its value - is the clearest example of what happens when a town's entire economy rests on one sector. When that sector contracts, there's nothing underneath holding the market up. A city or region with multiple employment drivers - healthcare, education, government, professional services, construction - absorbs shocks that a single-industry town cannot.

You can find this out without paying for a subscription or hiring a researcher. Search for the local government area and read what comes up - most Local Government Area (LGA) websites publish information about their economic profile, major employers, and infrastructure projects either underway or approved. If you want to go deeper, the Australian Bureau of Statistics (ABS) publishes employment and unemployment data by region. You are looking for two things: diverse employment and a trajectory that doesn't depend on one sector staying strong forever.

A word of caution here that applies to every layer of this research: there is no single source of truth. Check the data across more than one source. A number that appears in one report should be verified against another before you build a decision on it. This is not cynicism. It's discipline.

Then the suburb

This is where most couples start their research, and it is also where most of them get stuck - because suburb-level data is abundant, noisy, and easy to misread. The key is knowing what to look for and, equally, what to ignore.

A suburb that sits inside a genuine growth corridor will show several structural indicators: population growth that is sustained rather than spiking, proximity to employment nodes that are expanding, a healthy ratio of owner-occupiers to investors, and infrastructure investment that signals long-term government commitment - hospital upgrades, rail extensions, road projects, shopping centre redevelopments. These are not guarantees. But they are the fingerprints of structural demand, and structural demand is what sustains property values across cycles.

For historical capital growth and rental data, realestate.com.au is the most accessible starting point. CoreLogic's OnTheHouse platform provides suburb-level data on past sales and growth trends. SQM Research publishes useful free data on rental yields and vacancy rates. None of these tools will tell you what to buy. But they will tell you whether a suburb's recent performance is built on something structural or something temporary - and that distinction is what Matt discovered when he looked beneath Marsden Park's headline growth number.

Comparing suburbs for affordability is less straightforward. There is no free platform that does this well in a single view. The practical approach is to choose a local government area, look up the median prices for each suburb within it, and compare them manually. It is unglamorous work. It is also the work that separates the couple who buys well from the couple who buys fast. Microburbs is a useful resource that provides liveability data alongside property information, though the most detailed analysis sits behind a paywall.

Then the street

This is the layer that investors often skip, and it is frequently where the real risk hides. Two properties in the same suburb, three streets apart, can have fundamentally different risk profiles - and the difference is rarely visible from a listing photograph.

Flood zones, bushfire risk areas, flight paths, major road noise - these are the things that suppress long-term growth and make a property harder to rent and harder to sell. Most council LGA websites publish flood maps that you can search by address. For bushfire risk, the state planning authority will have overlay maps. For noise and other environmental factors, there is no substitute for standing on the street at different times of day. Ask the agent directly whether the property is affected by any known overlays or restrictions. A good agent will tell you. A great agent will show you the documentation.

School catchments matter more than most investors realise - not because you care which school the tenant's children attend, but because buyers care, and buyer demand is what drives capital growth over the long term. Every state government maintains a school catchment finder - search for 'school catchment' or 'school finder' followed by your state, enter the address, and you will know within minutes whether the property sits inside a high-demand catchment. This is five minutes of research that can materially affect a decade of returns.

Then the property itself

By the time you are looking at a specific property, most of the structural work is already done. The city is sound, the suburb is growing for the right reasons, and the street is clean of hidden risks. Now the question narrows: is this particular property worth owning for ten years?

Zoning is the first thing to check. The council LGA website will show you the current zoning for the property and any development applications lodged in the surrounding area. A large development approval next door can change a property's outlook overnight - sometimes for the better, sometimes dramatically for the worse. Your conveyancer can order a title search and planning certificate search for a modest fee, and this is money well spent before you commit to a purchase. It is far cheaper than discovering an easement or an overlay after settlement.

Comparable sales are your reality check on price. The sold section on realestate.com.au or Domain will show you what similar properties on the same street or in the same pocket have transacted for recently. This is not about finding the cheapest property. It is about knowing whether the price you are being asked to pay reflects the market or reflects the vendor's ambition.

And finally, the condition

Most couples feel confident with this because they can see and touch what they are assessing. Ironically, it is also where they are most likely to be misled - because a fresh coat of paint can hide a decade of neglect.

A pest and building inspection is not optional. It is the minimum. For older properties, a roof audit and an asbestos report should be added to the list. For units and apartments, the strata report is the single most revealing document you will read - it tells you the financial health of the building, the history of disputes, the planned maintenance, and the likelihood of special levies. A building that looks beautiful from the outside but has a depleted sinking fund and a history of deferred maintenance is a property that will cost you quietly for years.

For understanding what tenants and buyers in a particular area actually value - whether it is a second bathroom, a lock-up garage, north-facing orientation, or simply a third bedroom - the best source is not a website. It is a conversation with a local property manager. They see what tenants choose and what they reject, week after week. That ground-level intelligence is worth more than any amount of desktop research, and a ten-minute phone call will give you a clearer picture of tenant demand than hours spent on data platforms.

This five-layer approach is so much more than a formula; like every discipline in this book, its value is not in the individual steps, but in the behaviour it creates: the habit of looking beneath the surface before you commit, of verifying before you believe, and of trusting structure over excitement.

The Behaviour That Matters More Than the Property

The migrant families of post-war Sydney and Adam and Emily in modern Adelaide share one thing that the spreadsheets and market reports never quite capture: they both understood, eventually, that the property itself is not the decision. The decision is what you do after you buy it.

The couple who buys a good property and holds it with discipline for ten years will almost certainly outperform the couple who buys a great property and sells it after four years because something better came along, or because a rate rise made them nervous, or because a colleague told them the market had peaked.

Property rewards behaviour more than it rewards selection. A solid investment, held patiently, in an established suburb with structural demand, purchased at a price that fits within the couple's budget with a genuine margin of safety - that property doesn't need to be brilliant. It needs to be held.

The right property, in the end, is not the one that scores highest on the spreadsheet. It is the one that fits within your budget, lets you sleep at night, and sits quietly in the background building equity while you get on with the rest of your life.

That is not a compromise. That is the strategy.

WEALTH BUILDER REFLECTION

One question to sit with:
If rates rose two points, or the property sat vacant for two months, or the market went sideways for three years - could you still hold this property without stress? If not, what would need to change before you buy?

One truth to keep:

The right property is not the one that excites you most. It's the one you could hold through a hard year without needing to sell.

Chapter 4 asks the question that follows naturally: once you know what to buy, how do you fund it - and why does the sequence of that funding matter more than the speed?

CHAPTER 4

Funding Your Property Purchase

Sequence matters more than speed.

The broker had approved them for $780,000.

Nadia read the number on the screen and felt her chest tighten - not with excitement, but with the particular anxiety of having permission to do something enormous without being entirely sure how to do it well.

She was sitting in the study of their home in Caringbah, south of Sydney, with the loan pre-approval open on the laptop and a notepad covered in numbers that didn't quite add up. Ben was in the kitchen making coffee, but she could feel him listening through the doorway.

'We could use the offset,' she said. 'That gets us to a 20 per cent deposit on something around $650,000. Maybe a bit more.'

Ben came in with two mugs. 'Or we pull some equity from the house. The broker said we've got about $240,000 available.'

'So we use the equity as the deposit and keep the offset intact?'

'Or we use the offset for the deposit and set up a new equity line for renovations and buffer.'

'Or we do both and buy something bigger.'

They stared at each other. Two intelligent people with good incomes, a clear goal, and absolutely no idea which sequence of moves would put them in the strongest position. They had the resources. They had the borrowing power. What they didn't have - and what nobody had ever explained to them - was an order of operations.

Because in property investing, the order you do things in changes everything. Not slightly. Fundamentally. The same pool of money, deployed in a different sequence, produces a different tax outcome, a different risk profile, a different compounding trajectory, and a different level of financial flexibility five years down the track.

Nadia and Ben weren't short on capital. They were short on structure. And in the absence of structure, speed feels like progress. *It isn't.*

The couple who funds the right property in the wrong order often ends up worse off than the couple who waits three months and gets the sequence right.

The Myth

There is a moment in every property purchase where the couple has done the hard work - saved the deposit, built the equity, found the right property - and the final question is deceptively simple: *how do we pay for this?*

The answer feels obvious. You pull together the deposit, your conveyancer handles settlement, the vendor gets paid, and you own a property. What could possibly go wrong?

Quite a lot, as it turns out.

Most Australian couples fund their investment property the same way they funded their home: they accumulate savings, hand over a deposit, and sign a standard loan. The process feels familiar, and familiarity breeds a dangerous confidence that the same approach works for both.

It doesn't.

Your home loan and your investment loan serve fundamentally different purposes, receive fundamentally different tax treatment, and require fundamentally different structures. The couple who treats them the same -

who uses personal savings for an investment deposit when they could have borrowed the full amount, who pays down the investment loan when they should have been paying down the home loan, who mixes deductible and non-deductible debt because nobody told them not to - that couple is silently giving away thousands of dollars a year to the Australian Taxation Office (ATO). Not because they made a bad investment but because they funded a good investment in the wrong order.

This chapter is about sequence - the order in which you structure, fund, and hold a property investment. It is not about speed. Speed is what gets you into a property quickly. Sequence is what ensures you're still glad you bought it a decade from now.

Sequence matters more than speed. In every era, in every market, and for every couple who has ever built wealth with property.

WEALTH BUILDERS THROUGH TIME

The Shophouse Merchants of the Straits - Singapore and Penang, 1840–1920

In the mid-nineteenth century, a steady stream of Hokkien and Teochew migrants arrived in the British Straits Settlements - Singapore, Penang, and Malacca - with almost nothing. They had no capital. No connections. No family wealth that was waiting to be inherited. Most started as labourers, dock workers, or assistants in the shophouses that lined the commercial streets of the colonial ports.

Within two generations, a remarkable number of these families had built substantial property holdings, trading networks, and financial positions that endured well into the twentieth century. Their descendants became some of Southeast Asia's most prominent business families.

How they did it was no mystery. However, the method is what separated them sharply from the merchants - European, Malay, and Chinese alike - who arrived with more and ended up with less.

The Straits merchants operated on a principle that was rarely spoken but visible in every decision they made: *you do not skip steps*. Wealth is built in a sequence; each step must be secured before the next one begins.

This was not conservatism for its own sake. It was a discipline born from watching what happened to the merchants who jumped ahead; the trader who leased a warehouse before his shop was profitable; the speculator who bought land before he had steady income to service it; the ambitious young man who borrowed against future earnings to fund a partnership he could not yet afford... The Straits were littered with the wreckage of men who moved too fast.

The families who endured moved in a specific order, and didn't deviate from it.

The sequence was almost always the same: Firstly, a position in trade - a small shop, a market stall, a role within an existing merchant house that generated reliable income. This was the foundation. It was not glamorous, and it was not fast, but it was predictable. And predictable income was the precondition for everything that followed.

Second, the purchase of the shophouse itself - not a speculative plot of land on the city's fringe, but the building they already occupied. The building they already understood. They bought the asset that was already generating income, using the income it had already proven it could produce. The purchase was funded from accumulated trading profits, not borrowed ambition.

Third - and only once the shophouse was secured and the trade was stable - expansion. A second shophouse. A stake in a trading partnership. A share in a plantation venture. Each new commitment funded from the income of the previous one. Each step taken from a position of stability, never from a position of stretch.

The sequence was the strategy. Not the individual investments. The order.

The pressure to skip steps was enormous. Singapore and Penang in the 1860s and 1870s were boomtowns. Land prices were rising. Trading opportunities appeared and disappeared within months. The merchant who waited - who insisted on securing his current position before reaching for the next one - watched others leap ahead of him.

For a time, the ones making the leaps appeared to have got it right. The speculator who bought three properties on borrowed capital before his trade was profitable looked like a genius when prices rose. The young merchant who skipped the shophouse and went straight into plantation ownership looked visionary - until the commodity price turned, or the monsoon failed, or the credit was called in.

The disciplined families watched these collapses and recorded them - sometimes literally, in family ledgers and letters that survive today. They did not celebrate the failures of others. They simply noted what happened when the sequence was broken, and resolved, again, not to break it themselves.

By the early twentieth century, the families who had followed the sequence - trade, then property, then expansion, each step funded by the last - were among the most substantial property holders in the Straits Settlements. Their shophouse portfolios had compounded across decades. Their trading networks had been built on foundations that could absorb disruption. When the rubber price collapsed, when tin markets crashed, when political upheaval threatened the colonial order, these families had the reserves and the structure to endure what others could not.

The families who had skipped steps - who had moved fast, borrowed heavily, and trusted their timing over their structure - were, in most cases, gone. Not because they lacked talent or ambition. Because they had built the right things in the wrong order, and the order turned out to be the thing that mattered most.

The Straits merchants understood something that every generation of wealth builders eventually learns: speed and sequence feel like the same thing, but they are ultimately opposites. Speed is the urge to move before the foundation is set. Sequence is the discipline to build each layer on top of the last, and to refuse - no matter how strong the temptation - to skip a step that hasn't been earned.

The tools have changed. The principle hasn't.

An Australian couple in 2026 is not buying a shophouse in Singapore. But they are making the same structural decision those merchant families made 150 years ago: whether to fund their next move from a position of stability or a position of stretch; whether to get the sequence right or to get it fast.

A PRESENT-DAY STORY

The Couple Who Almost Left Money on the Table

Chris and Mei came to see me on a Thursday evening in late February, and within the first ten minutes it was clear they had already made up their minds. Chris was a physiotherapist with his own practice in Chatswood. Mei was a financial controller for a logistics company in North Sydney. Combined income around $265,000 - roughly $186,000 after tax, or about $15,500 a month hitting their accounts.

They owned their home in Epping - purchased five years earlier for $1.05 million, now worth roughly $1.35 million. Their home loan sat at about $780,000 after five years of principal and interest repayments at 6.2 per cent - costing them around $5,150 a month. The growth in their property was about $300,000, which at 80 per cent gave them roughly $240,000 in usable equity.

They had found a property they wanted to buy - a three-bedroom house in Kirwan, just outside Townsville, listed at $480,000. The numbers looked strong: similar houses in the area were renting for around $480 a week, and the suburb had the kind of steady demand from defence families and hospital workers that made for reliable tenancies. Their broker had told them they were approved. The agent wanted a decision by the end of the week. Everything was lined up.

They came to see me, wanting confirmation they were doing the right thing. What they were doing... was buying the right property in the wrong order.

Chris and Mei's plan was straightforward. They would withdraw $135,000 from their offset account and use it as the deposit on the Kirwan house. They'd take out an investment loan for the remaining $345,000. The house would be tenanted, the rent would cover most of the repayments, and the negative gearing benefit would handle the rest.

It sounded clean. It was actually expensive.

Here's what nobody had told them.

Their offset account was sitting against their home loan - a non-deductible debt. Every dollar in that offset was reducing interest on a loan they could not claim on their tax. The moment they withdrew that $135,000 and handed it to the vendor's settlement agent, their effective home loan balance would jump from $645,000 to $780,000 for interest calculation purposes. That meant roughly $8,400 more per year in non-deductible interest - money flowing to the bank that would generate zero tax benefit.

And here is what makes it so costly: the couple never feels it. Their monthly home loan repayment stays exactly the same - $5,150 a month, whether the offset holds $135,000 or nothing. What changes is what happens inside that repayment. With the offset in place, roughly $3,330 of each monthly payment goes to interest, and $1,820 goes to principal - money that builds equity in their home. Without the offset, roughly $4,030 goes to interest, and only

$1,120 goes to principal. Same bill. Same direct debit. But $700 a month quietly shifts from building their wealth to paying the bank - and because the repayment number on the statement never changes, most couples never notice it happened. The $8,400 a year doesn't arrive as a new bill. It arrives as equity they never built.

At the same time, they would have a smaller investment loan - $345,000 instead of $480,000 - which meant $8,775 less in deductible interest each year. At their marginal tax rate of 37 per cent, that was roughly $3,250 a year in tax deductions they were voluntarily giving up.

They were about to use tax-effective money to create a tax-ineffective outcome.

The alternative was not complicated. It just required doing things in a different order.

Instead of draining the offset for the deposit, Chris and Mei could borrow the full $480,000 as an investment loan, using the equity in their Epping home as additional security. The bank would cross-collateralise - using the home as security for the investment loan - but the two loans themselves would remain completely separate facilities: separate accounts, separate interest calculations, separate tax treatment. The home loan stays personal and non-deductible. The investment loan stays fully deductible. No mixing. No contamination.

I know what some readers are thinking, because Chris thought it too: using the family home as security for an investment feels risky. It feels like you're putting your home on the line. And I understand that instinct - it's a protective one coming from a good place.

But here is what matters more than the security structure: can you comfortably service both loans without stretching? Chris and Mei's investment loan at $480,000 on interest-only at 6.5 per cent would cost them $2,600 a month. On top of that sat the real costs of holding an investment property: property management fees at around 8 per cent of rent, council rates, landlord insurance, water charges, and a maintenance allowance - roughly $850 a month in total. The Kirwan house would bring in about $2,080 a month in rent, which left an out-of-pocket holding cost of around $1,370 a month before the tax benefit. After the negative gearing deduction flowed through at the higher earner's marginal rate, the real cost dropped to closer to $880 a month. On a combined take-home of $15,500 a month, with home loan repayments of $5,150, they still had comfortable room. They were not stretching. They were structuring.

The difference in tax position was clear. Under their original plan - offset drained, $345,000 investment loan - they would claim $22,425 a year in deductible interest. Under the restructured plan - offset intact, $480,000 investment loan - they would claim $31,200 a year. That's $8,775 more in deductible interest annually. At their marginal rate, that shift alone was worth roughly $3,250 a year in additional tax refund. And their offset account would keep reducing the non-deductible interest on their home loan, saving them another $8,400 a year compared to the drained scenario.

Same property. Same purchase price. Same household. But a fundamentally different structure - one that kept every dollar in its most tax-effective position.

Over a decade, the cumulative benefit of that structural difference was conservatively north of $30,000. Not from a better investment. Not from better timing. From doing the same thing in a different order.

Chris absorbed this information for a while. Clearly shocked at what was now an obvious equation. Then he asked the question most people ask at this point: why has nobody told me this before?

The honest answer is that the structure of an investment loan - how much to borrow, from where, in what order, against which security, and with what tax treatment - changes from couple to couple. It depends on income split, existing loan terms, offset balances, risk tolerance, and a dozen other variables that make every situation different. There is no one-size-fits-all answer, which is why it rarely gets explained in a general conversation with a banker or at an open inspection. It is the kind of decision that benefits from proper financial advice, or from years of studying how these structures actually work in practice. Most couples get neither, and so they default to the simplest path - which is almost never the most effective one.

Getting the sequence right meant slowing down. It meant going back to the broker, restructuring the loan application, setting up the investment facility as a separate account cross-collateralised against the home, and waiting for the paperwork to clear before they could proceed. It meant telling the agent they needed more time.

Chris wanted to move. The fear of losing the property was visceral. 'What if we miss it?' he asked.

Mei was quieter. She'd been running numbers on her phone while we talked. Eventually she looked up and said: 'If the right structure saves us $30,000, we can afford three weeks.'

Their conveyancer helped. She contacted the vendor's agent and negotiated a three-week extension on the finance clause, explaining that the buyers were restructuring their approval to proceed - not reconsidering the purchase. The vendor, who had already accepted the offer and didn't want to go back to market, agreed without much resistance. Agents create urgency because urgency closes deals. Conveyancers, when they're good, create the space to get the deal right.

Chris and Mei purchased the Kirwan house with the right structure in place - 100 per cent investment loan, cross-collateralised against the home, offset intact against the home loan, two completely separate facilities - and the difference in their cash flow was noticeable from the first month.

Two years after the purchase, Chris and Mei's position reflected the compounding effect of getting the sequence right from the start. Their offset account had continued to grow - they were adding to it regularly, and every dollar in it was reducing the non-deductible interest on their home loan. Their investment loan, meanwhile, was generating the maximum possible tax deduction because it represented the full cost of the asset.

The Kirwan house was performing well - tenanted consistently, growing steadily as Townsville's economic base strengthened, and generating a negative gearing benefit that was meaningfully larger than it would have been under the original plan. Their tax returns had shifted. Their cash flow was stronger. And they had begun directing the surplus toward a share investment that would become the second engine of their wealth-building system.

In our review meeting, Mei said she was glad they hadn't rushed. They'd had a plan, they'd had guidance, and the three weeks they'd spent restructuring before settlement had already paid for themselves several times over.

Chris and Mei bought the same property they would have bought three weeks earlier. They spent the same money. They took on the same debt. The only thing that changed was the order - the sequence in which the money moved and the structure that held it. That sequence, over a decade, was worth tens of thousands of dollars.

Getting the structure right before you buy is not caution. It is the single highest-return activity available to a couple at the point of purchase. Three weeks of patience. A decade of compounding benefit.

THE AUSTRALIAN APPLICATION

The Offset Account - Australia's Quiet Structural Gift

There is a financial tool available to almost every Australian mortgage holder; a tool that most of the world doesn't have, and that most Australians dramatically underuse. It is not complicated. It is not hidden. It is sitting in plain sight in the loan documentation that most couples signed without reading carefully.

The offset account.

Here is what it does, in plain English... An offset account is a transaction account linked to your mortgage. The balance in the offset is subtracted from your loan balance before the bank calculates your interest. If you owe $600,000 on your mortgage and you have $100,000 in your offset, the bank charges you interest on $500,000. The $100,000 is still yours - you can spend it, move it, use it at any time. But while it sits there, it is working as hard as a mortgage repayment without actually reducing your loan.

That distinction - reducing interest without reducing the loan - is the key to understanding why the offset account is so powerful for the couple who is building toward an investment property.

When you make extra repayments on your home loan, that money disappears into the mortgage. It reduces your balance, which reduces your interest, which is good. But if you later want to borrow for an investment, you need to redraw those extra repayments or refinance to access them - and here is where it gets expensive. Money redrawn from a home loan for investment purposes creates a mixed-purpose loan. The ATO does not allow you to claim the interest on the redrawn portion as a tax deduction in most circumstances, because the original loan was for a personal purpose and the redraw muddies the trail.

The offset avoids this entirely. Your loan balance stays at $600,000. Your offset balance sits at $100,000. You are paying interest on $500,000 - the same effective result as having made $100,000 in extra repayments - but the loan itself is untouched. Clean. Uncontaminated. Structurally ready for whatever comes next.

This is why every dollar Chris and Mei had saved into their offset was worth more there than it would have been as extra repayments on the mortgage. The interest saving was identical. But the flexibility was dramatically greater - not because they needed the offset for a deposit, but because the offset kept their non-deductible interest low while they borrowed the full investment amount separately. The offset was doing its job precisely by staying where it was.

For a dual-income couple building toward their first or second investment property, the offset account is not a 'nice-to-have'. It is the holding bay that keeps your non-deductible interest under control while your investment structure does the heavy lifting. It is where your emergency buffer lives. It is where you build liquidity for opportunities that cannot be geared - renovations, a share purchase, a one-off superannuation contribution. It is the part of your structure that gives you options without requiring you to restructure your debt.

And if you ever find yourself in a position where you cannot borrow the full amount for an investment property - perhaps the serviceability doesn't quite get there, or the lender's policy requires a cash deposit - then the offset is where that deposit comes from. It is less tax-effective than borrowing the full amount, but it is still better than making extra repayments and then trying to redraw. The offset keeps the money accessible and the loan structure clean, even when the ideal structure isn't available.

Most couples either don't have one, don't use it properly, or drain it at the point of purchase without understanding what they're giving up.

The offset account doesn't just save you interest. It preserves the structure that makes everything else work.

The Sequence That Matters

Here is the order of operations that the couples who get this right tend to follow. It is not the only way to fund an investment property. But it is the way that preserves the most flexibility, generates the most tax benefit, and creates the least structural damage over time.

1. They start with the home loan. Before they even begin looking for an investment property, they ensure their home loan is structured for what comes next. That means an offset account, not a redraw facility. It means understanding how much equity they have available above the 80 per cent threshold. It means having a conversation with a good broker about what the loan structure will look like when a second property enters the picture. This conversation costs nothing and saves thousands.

2. They build the deposit in the offset, not in a savings account and not as extra repayments. Every dollar saved into the offset reduces their home loan interest immediately while remaining fully accessible and structurally clean.

3. They borrow the full amount for the investment property wherever possible. The investment loan is set up as a completely separate facility - separate account, separate interest rate, separate tax treatment. If the bank requires security beyond the investment property itself, they cross-collateralise against the home. The security structure links the properties, but the loan accounts remain independent. That separation is non-negotiable, because it is what keeps the deductible and non-deductible interest cleanly apart.

   The investment loan is typically structured as interest-only, because the interest is fully tax-deductible and paying down the principal on a deductible loan while carrying non-deductible debt on the home is, to put it simply, paying the wrong mortgage first. Every spare dollar goes into the offset against the home loan, where it reduces the debt that generates no tax benefit. They keep the two debts entirely separate. No mixed-purpose accounts. No commingling of personal and investment funds. The cleaner the separation, the clearer the tax position, and the easier it is to manage, restructure, or sell one asset without unravelling the other.

4. They do all of this before they sign a contract. Not during settlement. Not after they've moved in a tenant. Before. Because restructuring a loan after the purchase is more expensive, more complex, and sometimes impossible without refinancing - which can trigger fees, revaluations, and the loss of existing rate arrangements.

The sequence is the strategy. The property is just the thing the strategy buys.

Why Speed Feels Like the Right Answer

It is worth naming why so many couples get this wrong, because the mistake is not stupidity. It is emotion.

Once a couple has decided to buy an investment property - once they have crossed the psychological threshold from thinking about it to acting on it - the urge to move quickly is almost irresistible. Every week they wait feels like a week of missed growth. Every property that sells to someone else feels like proof they should have moved faster. The agent's urgency, the broker's pre-approval, the rising prices in the suburb they've chosen - everything conspires to make speed feel like the responsible thing to do.

And speed, in fairness, has a real cost. Markets do move. Properties do sell. The couple who waits twelve months to get the perfect structure in place may genuinely miss a window.

But the cost of bad structure is almost always greater than the cost of moderate delay. A property that grows 5 per cent while you spend three weeks restructuring your loan has not cost you 5 per cent. It has cost you three weeks of that growth - a rounding error. A bad loan structure, compounding over a decade, can cost you multiples of that property's annual growth in lost tax deductions and unnecessary interest.

The Straits merchants knew this. The families who moved fast - who bought the next shophouse before the first one was secured, who expanded into plantations before their trade was stable - looked brilliant for a season. The families who moved in sequence looked slow. But fifty years later, the slow families owned the street.

There is a distinction that needs to be made here, because it is one that many couples use as an excuse without realising it. Waiting three weeks to get your loan structure right is not the same thing as waiting three years because you never quite got around to it. Sequence is a reason to pause briefly and build the right foundation. It is not a reason to stand still.

The couples I worry about most are not the ones who rush - they can usually be restructured and redirected. The ones I worry about are the couples who confuse patience with inaction. Who tell themselves they're 'getting everything in order' while months become years and the decision never gets made. Sequence means doing things in the right order. It does not mean doing nothing in the comfortable name of preparation.

Three weeks to restructure is discipline. Three years of research without a purchase is avoidance wearing the mask of prudence.

You don't need to buy faster. You need to buy in the right order. The order is worth more than the timing.

WEALTH BUILDER REFLECTION

One question to sit with:
If you had to explain - clearly, to each other - exactly how your next property purchase would be structured, which loan pays for what, and why the order matters, could you do it right now? And if not, is that a reason to wait three weeks or three years?

One truth to keep:

The deposit is not the hard part. The structure is. Get the structure right, and the property does the rest. Get it wrong, and you spend a decade paying for three weeks of impatience.

Chapter 5 takes a step back from the individual purchase and asks a bigger question: how do property markets actually move - and why does understanding the cycle give patient couples an advantage that no amount of timing ever will?

CHAPTER 5

Understanding Property Cycles

Long-term beats short-term

Angela was at her desk in the open-plan office of the accounting firm where she worked in Parramatta, coffee going cold beside the keyboard, when the email from the property manager loaded. *Routine portfolio revaluation.* Their Morningside house - three-bedroom Queenslander in Brisbane's inner east, bought eleven months ago for $685,000, their first investment property. They had spent two years saving for it, and six months finding it.

Current estimated value: $648,000.

She read the number twice. Then a third time, slowly, as though the digits might rearrange themselves into something less brutal. They didn't. She sat very still. Around her, the office continued - phones ringing, someone laughing in the kitchen, the mundane noise of a Tuesday morning - and none of it reached her.

She didn't forward the email to Dean. She rang him. He picked up from the car park of the construction site in Penrith where he was supervising a fit-out. She could hear the wind against his phone.

'The revaluation for Morningside came in,' she said. 'We're down thirty-seven thousand.'

A pause, with only the sound of the wind. Then: 'Since when?'

'Since we bought it. Eleven months ago.'

Neither of them spoke for a few seconds. It was the particular silence of two people recalculating something they had believed was settled.

That night, at the kitchen table of their home in Merrylands, they opened the laptop and did what every couple does when a number frightens them. They searched for proof that it was going to get worse.

They found it immediately. Articles about Brisbane oversupply in certain corridors. Commentary about interest rate uncertainty. A property forum where someone had posted, with the unearned authority of an anonymous screen name, that Brisbane was 'at least eighteen months from a bottom.'

Dean closed the laptop. 'We should sell. Before it gets worse.'

Angela didn't look at him. 'We've owned it for eleven months. We haven't even had a full summer of rent.'

'So we wait until it drops another fifty thousand?'

'How do you know it will?'

'How do you know it won't?'

They went to bed without resolving it. Angela lay in the dark and felt the weight of a number she had seen twelve hours ago pressing against her ribs like something physical. She wasn't afraid of thirty-seven thousand dollars. She was afraid that the decision they had been most proud of - the one they had told their parents about, the one that was supposed to be the start of something - might have been a mistake.

That fear - the quiet, 3 am fear that you got it wrong - is the subject of this chapter. Not because the fear is rational. But because what you do with it determines everything that happens next.

The market is not doing something to you. It is doing something it has always done. The only question is whether you knew to expect it.

Australian property does not move in a straight line. Everyone knows this in the abstract. Very few people feel it in the gut until they are lying awake at 1 am doing arithmetic on a valuation that arrived that morning.

There are two entirely different ways to experience a property market. The first is reactive. You buy when prices are rising because the momentum makes the decision feel safe. You panic when prices flatten or fall because the absence of growth feels like failure. You check comparable sales obsessively. You treat each quarterly movement as a verdict on your intelligence.

The second way is structural. You understand that property markets move through long, repeating phases - and that the specific timing of each phase is unpredictable but the existence of the pattern is not. You bought knowing that a flat year was not a risk to be avoided but a certainty to be absorbed. You hold because your structure can withstand it, not because you believe prices will rise tomorrow.

The first couple sells at the worst possible moment. The second couple is still holding when the growth arrives.

The flat years aren't the cost of owning property. They're the price of admission to growth.

WEALTH BUILDERS THROUGH TIME

The Families Who Bought the Fear - Hong Kong, 1967–1997

In the spring of 1967, Hong Kong was burning. Riots had erupted across Kowloon and the New Territories - strikes, bombings, running battles in the streets of North Point and Wong Tai Sin - inspired by the Cultural Revolution raging across the border in mainland China. The colonial government imposed curfews. Foreign businesses began evacuating staff.

Families who could afford to leave queued at Kai Tak airport with suitcases and one-way tickets to London, Vancouver, and Sydney.

Property prices collapsed. Residential flats in Mid-Levels that had traded at HK$30 per square foot fell below HK$15. Commercial buildings in Tsim Sha Tsui sat empty. Construction sites across the harbour were abandoned mid-pour, bamboo scaffolding still clinging to half-finished towers. The conventional wisdom, spoken openly in the lobbies of Central's banking houses, was that Hong Kong was finished.

It was, in fact, the beginning of one of the most extraordinary property stories in modern history.

A small number of families - many of them Shanghai industrialists who had already survived one upheaval when they fled the mainland in 1949 - held a belief that separated them from the departing crowd. They did not believe Hong Kong was immune to crisis. They believed the opposite: that crisis was part of the pattern. That property in a land-scarce, harbour-locked, economically vital port city would always recover, because the forces driving demand - population, commerce, geography - were structural. The crisis was temporary. The scarcity was permanent.

They had seen this before in Shanghai, where fortunes had been made and lost and made again across decades of political upheaval. The pattern was familiar. Fear emptied the market. Patience refilled it. The family that could endure the emptying inherited the refilling.

While others sold, these families bought. Not recklessly - carefully, methodically, with capital preserved from manufacturing businesses they had continued to operate through the unrest. They purchased residential blocks in Mid-Levels and Kowloon Tong. They acquired commercial sites in Wan Chai. They bought from departing owners at prices that reflected the panic, not the fundamentals - paying a fraction of what the same buildings had traded for eighteen months earlier.

Then they waited.

The recovery was not immediate. The late 1960s and early 1970s were a slow grind upwards, punctuated by a sharp correction in 1973–74 when a global oil crisis and a local stock market collapse sent property values down again. The families who had bought at the bottom of the 1967 panic watched their holdings fall a second time within six years.

They held.

The tension was not merely financial. It was existential. Hong Kong's political future was genuinely uncertain. The lease on the New Territories would expire in 1997. Mainland China's intentions were opaque. At every point in the cycle - every correction, every political tremor, every headline about the colony's fragile future - there was a compelling, rational reason to sell and leave.

And every time, a wave of sellers transferred their property to a smaller group of patient buyers. There were the 1967 riots, then the 1973 crash. This was followed by the uncertainty of the early 1980s as the Sino-British negotiations began. The Tiananmen shock of 1989 came after that, with the handover anxiety of the mid-1990s. Each crisis had its own character. Each felt, to the people living through it, unprecedented and permanent. And each was followed by a recovery that exceeded the previous peak.

The families who stayed did not stay because they were certain. They stayed because they recognised the shape of what was happening. They had seen it before - in Shanghai, in the previous cycle, in the cycle before that. The emotion was new each time. The pattern was not.

By the early 1990s, the families who had bought through the crises of the previous three decades held some of the most valuable property portfolios in Asia. A Mid-Levels apartment block purchased for HK$200,000 in the aftermath of 1967 was worth tens of millions. The commercial sites acquired during the 1974 correction had become the foundations of development empires that would shape the Hong Kong skyline.

The families who had sold during those same crises - who had read the headlines, felt the fear, and converted appreciating property into depreciating cash - had locked in the loss at the bottom and missed the recovery at the top. Not because they were foolish. Because they were experiencing the cycle for the first time and mistaking it for the end.

What the great Hong Kong property families understood was not the timing of cycles; they couldn't predict when the market would turn any more than anyone else. What they understood was the *shape* - the pattern itself. Fear at the bottom. Greed at the top. And the quiet, undramatic middle where the real wealth is built by the people who refuse to leave.

The greatest advantage in property is not information, the structural ability to do nothing when everything around you is screaming to act.

The tools have changed. The principle hasn't.

An Australian couple watching a Brisbane valuation fall is not holding apartment blocks in Kowloon. But they are feeling the same fear, at the same point in the same pattern, that every property investor in every city has felt for centuries. The question is whether they recognise it.

A PRESENT-DAY STORY

The Couple Who Held Through the Silence

Kate and Sam had done everything right. That is how it felt in early 2017 when they purchased their first investment property - a solid three-bedroom house in Logan, south of Brisbane - for $385,000. Kate was a speech pathologist working across two clinics in the Redlands. Sam managed procurement for a mid-tier engineering firm. Combined income around $205,000. They had structured the purchase carefully: equity release from their home in Cleveland for the deposit, separate investment loan, offset intact.

The property was tenanted within two weeks. The rent covered the interest and most of the holding costs. The negative gearing benefit flowed through their tax returns. Everything was moving in the right direction.

Then Brisbane's property market went quiet. And it stayed quiet for three years.

They had bought deep into a long, flat period in Brisbane property. While Sydney and Melbourne had surged through 2015 and 2016, Brisbane had barely moved. The expectation - theirs, their broker's, most commentators' - was that Brisbane was next. The gap between Sydney and Brisbane prices was historically wide. The fundamentals were strong. The growth was 'overdue.'

It didn't come. Not in 2017. Not in 2018. Not in 2019. The Logan property sat at roughly the same value for nearly three years while friends and colleagues in Sydney watched their homes appreciate by hundreds of thousands of dollars. Sam's sister had bought a two-bedroom apartment in Surry Hills the same month they had bought in Logan. Hers had grown $140,000. Theirs had grown nothing.

Sam started questioning the purchase. Not angrily - she was too measured for that - but quietly, persistently, in the half-hour after their daughter was in bed when the doubts had room to breathe. 'Should we have bought in Sydney instead? Should we sell and redirect into shares? Are we just sitting on dead money?'

Kate listened. She didn't have certainty. But she had done something Sam hadn't yet: she had looked at the data.

It started on a Sunday afternoon while Sam was at the park with their daughter. Kate opened SQM Research - a free online platform that publishes vacancy rates, rental yields, and asking prices for every suburb and region in

Australia - and began pulling numbers for Logan and the surrounding corridors. Then she did the same for Sydney, Melbourne, and Perth, dropping the figures into a spreadsheet side by side. The question was simple: where are the imbalances?

What came back confirmed what she had suspected but hadn't been able to articulate. Logan's vacancy rate was sitting at 1.2 per cent. Sydney's was above 3 per cent. Melbourne's was climbing. The rental yield on their Logan house was over 5 per cent - well above the national average, and nearly double what a comparable property in Sydney would return. The rent hadn't dropped. Their tenant hadn't left. The demand for housing in Logan hadn't gone anywhere. The only thing that had disappeared was the price growth - and the data was telling her that this was temporary, because the fundamentals beneath the price were tightening, not loosening.

She went further. She pulled Brisbane's historical price data and laid it alongside the vacancy and yield numbers going back twenty years. The pattern was so consistent it was almost boring. Every time vacancy rates fell below 2 per cent, and yields climbed above the national average, the growth phase followed. Sometimes within a year. Sometimes two. But it inevitably followed. Brisbane had done this in the early 2000s. It had done it again before the 2006–2008 surge. And the numbers were doing it now.

That evening, she showed Sam the screen. Not a forecast. Not an opinion piece. Two numbers - vacancy and yield - across four cities, with twenty years of history sitting beside them.

'The rent is strong. The vacancy is low. The demand is there,' Kate said. 'The only thing that hasn't moved is the price. And every time the data has looked like this, the price has followed.'

This is the part most people never learn, and it is remarkably simple. You do not need to predict property cycles. You need to read two numbers: *vacancy rates* and *rental yields*. When vacancy is tightening, and yields are above average - at the state level or the suburb level - demand is outstripping supply, and the market is coiling. That is the quiet phase before the growth. The data is free. SQM Research publishes it weekly. CoreLogic tracks it monthly. An AI tool can compare the ratios across every capital city in minutes. The couple who checks these numbers once a quarter will never be blindsided by a cycle again. They won't predict the timing - but they will know the direction.

It was the hardest kind of decision - the decision to hold a position when nothing visible is confirming that you're right. No price growth to validate the purchase. No movement to reward the patience. Just the quiet, unglamorous act of paying a mortgage on a property that hadn't moved, month after month, while the world seemed to be rewarding everyone except them. But beneath the stillness, the numbers were moving. Kate could see it. And now, so could Sam.

Then came March 2020. Kate remembers the Tuesday evening it became real. The Prime Minister was on television. Borders were closing. The ASX had fallen 30 per cent in three weeks. Sam came home from what turned out to be her last day in the office for four months and sat down at the kitchen table without taking off her jacket.

'How bad is this going to get?' she said.

Kate didn't know. Nobody did. Their tenant had called that morning to ask, carefully, whether they could delay rent by two weeks if it came to that. The property manager was sending updates that read like dispatches from a war zone. Other landlords were offering rent reductions. Some were losing tenants entirely.

Sam's sister in Sydney had already sold her Surry Hills apartment. Locked in her $140,000 gain before the market fell further, she said.

For three nights, Kate and Sam had the same conversation: different words each time, but the same conversation.

'Should we sell?'

'To whom? In this market, who's buying a house in Logan?'

'So we just sit here.'

'We sit here.'

They sat. The tenant paid rent, two weeks late but in full. The mortgage came out automatically. The offset absorbed the buffer. The world outside felt like it was coming apart, and inside their kitchen in Cleveland, two people were doing the most difficult and most profitable thing an investor can do.

Nothing.

Brisbane's property market turned in late 2020. What followed was one of the sharpest growth periods in Australian property history. Interstate migration from Sydney and Melbourne, driven by remote work and relative affordability, poured demand into a market that had been flat for half a decade. Supply was constrained. Prices moved fast.

The Logan house they had bought for $385,000 - the one that had sat stubbornly still for three years, the one that had been revalued at $372,000 at its lowest point, the one that Sam's parents had gently suggested they cut their losses on - was valued at $520,000 by mid-2021. By early 2023, it had crossed $610,000.

Sam's sister, who had sold her Sydney apartment to 'lock in gains,' watched the Sydney market surge past her sale price within eight months. She had traded a compounding asset for a number in a bank account that was quietly losing value to inflation. She had felt decisive. She had been reactive.

Sam said something in our next review that I have thought about many times since: 'Everyone talks about the big moves. The bold trades. The smart timing. The most money we've ever made was by sitting at a kitchen table, doing absolutely nothing.'

Kate and Sam did not predict Brisbane's boom. They did not predict COVID. They did not time anything. They bought a solid property in an established suburb at a reasonable price, and they held it through a full cycle - the flat years, the dip, the crisis, and the recovery.

The growth didn't arrive because Brisbane was special. It arrived because cycles always complete. The only question was whether Kate and Sam would still be holding the property when it did.

THE AUSTRALIAN APPLICATION

Time Is Literally Rewarded by Law

There is a structural advantage built into the Australian tax system that most couples have heard of, but few have truly absorbed. It is the way capital gains are taxed - and it is, quietly, one of the most powerful reasons to hold a property investment through a full cycle rather than selling at the first sign of either trouble or profit.

Here is how it has worked, in plain language. When you sell an investment property for more than you paid for it, the profit is a capital gain, and you owe tax on it. That tax is calculated at your marginal rate - the same rate you pay on your salary. For most dual-income couples, that rate is somewhere between 30 and 45 cents in the dollar. A significant chunk of the profit going straight to the ATO.

For decades, Australia offered a straightforward reward for patience: if you held the asset for at least twelve months before selling, the ATO halved the taxable gain. A $200,000 profit became $100,000 of taxable income. At a marginal rate of 37 per cent, that was the difference between a $74,000 tax bill and a $37,000 one. Thirty-seven thousand dollars, kept in your pocket, for the act of holding.

At the time of writing, the government has proposed replacing the 50 per cent discount with an indexation method, effective from 1 July 2027. Under indexation, instead of halving the gain, you adjust your original purchase price upward by inflation - the Consumer Price Index - for every year you held the property. The effect is that the tax system strips out the portion of your gain that was merely inflation and only taxes the real growth. The proposal also includes a 30 per cent minimum effective tax on the real gain - meaning that even with indexation, you will pay at least 30 cents in the dollar on the growth above inflation.

Here is what that looks like in practice. Say you bought a property for $500,000 and sold it ten years later for $750,000. Under the old discount method, your $250,000 gain would be halved to $125,000 of taxable income. Under indexation, if inflation averaged three per cent over that decade, your cost base would be adjusted to roughly $672,000. Your taxable gain would be $78,000 - lower than the discount method for long holds, because each additional year of holding pushes the cost base higher.

The specific method may change. The principle does not. Whether the system halves your gain or adjusts your cost base for inflation, the structural incentive points in the same direction: hold. The longer you hold, the less tax you pay on the growth. The tax system is not neutral on the question of patience. It actively rewards it.

For a dual-income couple, the benefit compounds further regardless of which method applies. If the property is held jointly, the capital gain is split between two people - each paying tax at their own marginal rate (if more than 30% in the new method). If one partner earns less than the other, their share of the gain is taxed at a lower rate. The structure of the couple itself becomes a tax advantage, layered on top of whatever discount or indexation benefit they receive for holding.

The tax system does not reward the couple who times the market. It rewards the couple who has the patience to sit through it.

What Angela and Dean Found When They Ran the Numbers

Six months after the valuation that shook them, Angela did something she should have done on the night Dean first said 'sell.' She stopped reading property forums. She opened a spreadsheet. And she ran the actual cost of selling.

Angela was an accountant. Numbers were her language. She had spent six months reacting to a number - the $37,000 paper loss - without ever putting it in context. Now she did.

Agent's commission on a $648,000 sale: roughly $16,000. Marketing campaign: $6,000. Conveyancing and legal fees: $2,000. They had held for less than twelve months, so no CGT discount or indexation benefit would apply - not that it mattered, since there was no gain. Total cost of exiting the property: approximately $24,000 in hard cash, on top of the $37,000 they had already lost on paper. Selling would not cost them thirty-seven thousand dollars. It would cost them more than sixty thousand.

And if they wanted to reinvest later - to buy back into Brisbane after the market recovered, the way buyers always do - they would pay stamp duty on the new purchase. Another $15,000 to $25,000, depending on the price. The total cost of panic, converted into dollars: somewhere between $75,000 and $85,000.

She put the spreadsheet in front of Dean that Saturday morning without commentary. He read it the way she had read the valuation email six months earlier - slowly, then again, then a third time.

The property was costing them, in real after-tax terms, less than $80 a week to hold. The tenant was reliable. The rental income covered the interest. The negative gearing benefit was reducing their tax. The offset on their home loan was still growing—eighty dollars a week against an $85,000 exit cost. The arithmetic wasn't close.

Dean closed the spreadsheet. Neither of them said anything worth quoting. There was no moment of revelation, no sentence that captured the principle in a single breath. There were just two people looking at the same numbers and arriving at the same conclusion at the same time.

They held.

Sometimes the most important financial decision a couple makes doesn't feel like a decision at all. It feels like arithmetic.

WEALTH BUILDER REFLECTION

One question to sit with:
If the property you own - or the one you're about to buy - didn't move for three years, would your structure hold? And would your nerve?

One truth to keep:
The flat years aren't the cost of owning property. They're the price of admission to the growth. Every couple who built lasting wealth in property paid that price. The ones who refused to pay it are the ones who sold.

Chapter 6 takes the principle of patience one step further and asks: what does the Australian tax system actually give you for holding property - and why do most couples leave tens of thousands of dollars on the table without realising it?

CHAPTER 6

Tax Benefits of Property

Structure > tactics

It is a Tuesday evening in April, and Rebecca is standing at the kitchen bench in Kellyville with her phone in one hand and a glass of wine in the other.

The email from their accountant is not bad news. It is a notice of assessment - a refund of $4,200 from the previous financial year. She should be pleased. Instead, she is staring at the screen with the expression of someone who suspects they are being short-changed but cannot prove it.

Lachlan walks in from the garage, sees her face, and stops

'What's up?'

'My return came through. Four thousand two hundred.'

'Mine came through this morning. Just under two thousand.'

Rebecca does the arithmetic without looking up. Six thousand between them. She puts the phone on the bench and picks up her wine.

'I was having coffee with Olivia at work today. She and Nav bought an investment property last year - roughly the same price as ours, roughly the same income as us. She said Nav got back about seven thousand on his return and she got back four. Between them, about eleven thousand.'

Lachlan leans against the bench. 'Maybe they have a better accountant.'

'Maybe. Or maybe we're set up wrong.'

They are not set up wrong, exactly. They are set up incompletely. And the difference between those two things, for an Australian dual-income couple, is worth tens of thousands of dollars across the life of a single investment property.

This is a chapter about what the Australian tax system actually gives you for owning an investment property - and why most couples collect a fraction of what they are entitled to. Not because the benefits are hidden, but because nobody ever sat them down and explained how the pieces fit together.

Most Australian couples know that investment property comes with tax benefits. They have heard the phrase 'negative gearing' at barbecues, read about depreciation in a weekend property supplement, and have a vague sense that the government gives you something back for owning a rental.

But vague is expensive.

The couple who understands the structure of these benefits - not the fine print, the structure - makes different decisions at every stage. They buy differently. They finance differently. They claim differently. And over a decade, the gap between a vaguely aware couple and a structurally informed one is not marginal. It is transformative.

The tension in this chapter is not between knowledge and ignorance. It is between tactics and structure. The couple chasing individual tax tips - a depreciation claim here, an interest deduction there - will always be playing catch-up to the couple who understands how the entire system works as a single, integrated advantage.

Structure beats tactics. This is the chapter where that principle earns its weight.

WEALTH BUILDERS THROUGH TIME

The Venetian Landlords - Venice, 1400–1600

In the fifteenth century, Venice was the wealthiest city in Europe - a maritime republic built on trade, banking, and a political system designed to protect the interests of its propertied families. The Venetian elite did not simply own property. They operated inside a system of laws, customs, and tax structures that made property ownership one of the most powerful wealth-preservation tools in the Mediterranean world.

The Republic's fiscal structure favoured the property-owning class. Trade was heavily taxed through customs duties and shipping levies; property ownership came with stable rights, predictable assessment, and legal protections that compounded over generations.

The Venetian families who understood this did not treat property as a passive asset. They treated it as a structural position within a system designed to favour them. They saw what their contemporaries in other Italian city-states often missed: that the way you held an asset mattered as much as the asset itself. A palazzo generating rental income was not just a building. It was a tax-advantaged vehicle inside a system that rewarded the holder for doing exactly what the state needed done.

The great Venetian families - the Contarini, the Mocenigo, the Corner - systematically acquired income-producing property across the city and the surrounding terraferma. They did not chase the most beautiful buildings or the highest rents. They built portfolios that maximised the structural advantages the Venetian system offered: favourable tax treatment on rental income, protection of property rights across generations, and access to low-cost credit secured against their holdings.

They structured their wealth around the system, not against it.

The temptation for Venetian merchants was always maritime trade. The margins were spectacular - a single successful voyage to Constantinople or Alexandria could return five or ten times the investment. But the risks were equally spectacular. Ships sank. Cargoes were seized. Wars closed trade routes overnight. The families who poured everything into trade could become fabulously wealthy in a single decade and entirely ruined in the next.

The property-owning families watched this happen with the regularity of tides. And they held their position.

The Venetian landlord families endured for centuries. Not because property never lost value - Venice experienced floods, plagues, and economic contractions that shook every asset class. But because the structure of ownership - the tax advantages, the legal protections, the intergenerational transfer mechanisms - created a compounding advantage that grew wider with every decade.

By the sixteenth century, the wealthiest families in Venice were not the traders. They were the families who had used trade profits to acquire property, and then allowed the structural advantages of property ownership to compound across generations. Their wealth had shifted from active to structural - from something they earned to something the system sustained.

The Venetian insight was not that property was a good investment. Everyone knew that. The insight was that the system surrounding property - the tax code, the legal framework, the financing structures - was itself a source of return. The families who understood this built differently from the families who simply bought well.

They did not work harder than their peers. They just worked inside a structure that multiplied the value of every decision they made.

The tools have changed. The principle hasn't.

An Australian couple in 2026 does not own a Venetian palazzo. But they operate inside a tax system that is, in its own way, just as deliberately structured to reward the property holder who understands it. Negative gearing, depreciation, interest deductions, offset accounts - these are not scattered benefits. They are an integrated system. And the couple who sees the system, rather than the individual pieces, will build wealth the way the Venetian landlords did: not by working harder, but by working inside a structure designed to reward exactly what they are doing.

A PRESENT-DAY STORY

The Couple Who Left Money on the Floor

Daniel was an electrician running his own small business on the Central Coast. Meg was a primary school teacher in Gosford. Between them, they earned around $205,000 - Daniel's income variable depending on the year, averaging around $130,000 but spiking to $145,000 in a busy one; Meg's steady at $75,000. They had bought their home in Woy Woy five years earlier with a loan of around $420,000. They had one investment property - a two-bedroom unit in Newcastle they had purchased eighteen months ago for $485,000, with a 20 per cent deposit and an investment loan of $388,000.

The Newcastle unit was tenanted and returning $450 a week in rent. The investment loan was on principal and interest repayments - because Daniel believed in paying down debt, all debt, as fast as possible. They also had $85,000 sitting in an offset account linked to the investment loan, because it was the bigger loan and Daniel's instinct was to attack it first. After interest, principal, strata, insurance, property management, and council rates, the property was costing them a fair bit each week. But the loan was shrinking. The offset was chipping away. It felt like progress.

Their accountant was solid. Depreciation was being claimed - both capital works on the building and the diminishing value of the fixtures. Interest, management fees, strata, insurance, rates - all lodged correctly. At tax time, the negative gearing benefit came through at around $5,800 across both returns. It helped. But it didn't change anything.

Daniel and Meg believed what most property investors believe in their first few years: that the tax benefit was the tax benefit. The accountant was doing the work. The deductions were being claimed. The offset was reducing the biggest loan. The principal was coming down. There was nothing more to do.

What they didn't understand was that their accountant was doing the right job - but the structure underneath it was working against them. In two ways.

The offset was in the wrong place.

Their investment loan was $388,000. With $85,000 in offset sitting against it, they were only paying interest on $303,000. That felt responsible. But every dollar of interest on an investment loan is tax-deductible. By reducing that interest with the offset, they were shrinking the very deduction the tax system was designed to give them. They were paying less interest on the loan they could claim - and more interest on the one they couldn't.

Meanwhile, their home loan - $420,000 of non-deductible debt - had no offset at all. Every dollar of interest on that loan was a pure cost. No deduction. No benefit. Just money leaving the household with nothing coming back from the tax system.

By parking $85,000 against the wrong loan, they were forgoing roughly $5,100 a year in deductible interest they could have claimed on the investment - and paying roughly $5,100 a year in non-deductible interest on their home that they didn't need to.

And the repayment structure was compounding the problem.

Every principal and interest repayment on the investment loan was reducing the balance of their deductible debt. That sounds like a good thing. It isn't - not when the other loan in the household is non-deductible. Every dollar of principal they paid down on the investment was a dollar that could have gone toward the home loan instead - reducing the debt that gave them no tax benefit while preserving the debt that did.

A conversation with a financial planner changed the trajectory. Not because the planner knew secrets. Because the planner could see the system - not just the tax return, but the architecture underneath it.

1. The first structural change was simple: *move the funds in the offset.* Detach it from the investment loan and reattach it to the home loan (this is allowed as long as the funds were saved and not borrowed

initially). The $85,000 would now sit against the non-deductible debt, immediately reducing the interest on the loan they couldn't claim. The investment loan would return to its full balance, and the interest - now higher - would be fully deductible against their income. The total interest paid across both loans was almost identical. But the split between deductible and non-deductible had shifted dramatically in their favour.

2. The second change was the repayment type. The planner switched the investment loan from principal and interest to interest only. This stopped them from paying down deductible debt - debt the tax system was rewarding them for holding. The principal component they had been directing toward the investment, roughly $90 a week, was redirected as extra repayments on the home loan instead. Same money leaving the household. But now it was reducing the loan that cost them the most after tax.
3. The third change was a PAYG withholding variation. Most couples wait twelve months for their negative gearing refund to arrive as a lump sum from the ATO. But the system allows you to apply for a variation so the benefit flows through your pay cycle - less tax withheld each fortnight, more cash in hand every payday. The planner advised the clients to lodge the application, and within weeks, Daniel and Meg were receiving an extra $230 a fortnight in their combined take-home pay. The same benefit, delivered when it was useful rather than when the ATO got around to processing it. That money went straight into the offset against the home loan, where it immediately began reducing their non-deductible interest further.
4. The fourth element was forward-looking. The planner walked them through the ownership structure for their next investment property. In the years Daniel's income pushed above $135,000, his marginal tax rate on those dollars climbed from 30 to 37 cents. If their next property were held in his name alone, the deductible losses would

flow entirely through his return at the higher marginal rate - delivering a meaningfully larger tax benefit than a fifty-fifty split. This wasn't something they could change on the Newcastle unit. It was something they could build into the next one from day one.

The tension was not financial. It was psychological. Everything the planner was recommending ran against Daniel's instincts. Move the offset away from the bigger loan. Stop paying down the investment. Let the deductible debt sit there, untouched, while you attack the home loan instead. The out-of-pocket holding cost on the investment, which had felt manageable, would jump noticeably. It felt like going backwards on every front.

Meg saw it differently. 'We're not paying more in total. We're just paying more on the loan we get taxed for and less on the one we don't. The money's going to the same place - it's just working harder.'

She was right. But it took Daniel three weeks to make the call to the bank.

In the first full financial year after the restructure, their household position improved by more than $9,000. The tax refund increased from the larger deductible interest. The non-deductible interest on the home loan dropped from the restored offset. The extra repayments from the interest-only switch accelerated the home loan paydown. And the PAYG variation put cash back in their hands each fortnight instead of once a year - cash that went straight into the offset, compounding the benefit. The property had not changed. The rent had not changed. The total debt had not changed. What had changed was which loan the offset sat against, which loan they were paying down, and how the tax benefit reached them - three structural shifts that redirected thousands of dollars a year from the ATO's pocket into theirs.

Over the following three years, the restructured position delivered a cumulative improvement of more than $30,000. Money that reduced the home loan, strengthened the offset, and accelerated the build-up of their next deposit.

On the drive home from the planner's office after the restructure was finalised, Daniel was quiet for a long time. Then he said to Meg: 'Same bricks. Same loan. We just built better walls around them.'

Daniel and Meg did not need a better investment. They needed a better structure around the investment they already had. The property was always capable of delivering those benefits. The tax system was always designed to provide them. What was missing was not ambition or intelligence. It was architecture.

The couple who understands the structure doesn't just save on tax. They redirect that saving into the next asset, the next deposit, the next layer of the system. Tax efficiency is not an outcome. It is a compounding input.

THE AUSTRALIAN APPLICATION

Negative Gearing Is Not What You Think It Is

Most Australians have heard of negative gearing. Fewer understand it. And almost nobody talks about what it actually does inside a dual-income household.

Here is the plain version. When the total costs of holding an investment property - interest, management, insurance, council rates, depreciation, repairs - exceed the rental income the property generates, the property is negatively geared. It is running at a loss. And under Australian tax law, that loss can be deducted directly from your personal income. Not from a separate investment account. Not from a theoretical tax bucket. From your salary. From the income you go to work for every day.

For a couple earning $240,000 combined - say one partner on $150,000 and the other on $90,000 - with a negatively geared investment property generating $18,000 in deductible losses, the benefit is substantial. The partner on $150,000 has a marginal tax rate of 37 cents on income above $135,000. If $9,000 of that loss flows through their return, the tax saving on the portion above the $135,000 threshold is calculated at 37 cents in the dollar. The partner on $90,000, in the 30 per cent bracket, saves at 30 cents. The combined benefit can easily exceed $6,000 in a single financial year.

But here is the part most couples never act on. The ATO allows you to apply for a PAYG withholding variation, which reduces the tax taken from your salary across the year. Instead of waiting twelve months for a $6,000 refund, you receive roughly $230 extra in your combined pay each fortnight. The money arrives when it is useful - not when the ATO gets around to processing your return.

This is the kind of structural knowledge that separates the couple who feels like their investment property is a burden from the couple who feels like the system is working with them. The benefit is identical in both cases. The experience of it is entirely different.

And here is the part that most couples never hear: *negative gearing is not permanent.* As rents rise over time - and across every long-term dataset, Australian rents rise - the gap between rental income and holding costs narrows. A property that is negatively geared in year one may be neutrally geared by year five and positively geared by year eight. The tax benefit transitions naturally from a direct deduction to a cash-flow positive asset. The couple has been supported by the system during the building years and rewarded by the market during the growth years.

What the 2026 Budget Means for Property Investors

As this book goes to print, the Federal Government's 2026–27 Budget has proposed significant changes to negative gearing for residential property. From 1 July 2027, investors who purchase established residential properties after Budget night - 7:30 pm on 12 May 2026 - will no longer be able to deduct net rental losses against their salary or other personal income. Instead, those losses will only be deductible against income from residential property. Excess losses can be carried forward.

Three things are worth understanding clearly. First, existing properties are grandfathered. If you already own an investment property, or had exchanged contracts before the government announced the Budget changes on 12th May 2026, the current rules continue to apply. Your negative gearing benefit is unchanged. Second, new builds are exempt. Investors who purchase eligible newly constructed properties will retain full access to negative gearing. The Government's stated intention is to redirect investment toward new housing supply. Third, these changes are proposed, not yet legislated. They require passage through Parliament and may be amended.

What does this mean for the structural principle in this chapter? It reinforces it. The couple who understands the system - who pays attention to how the rules are changing, not just what the rules were - will adapt. They may weigh future purchases toward new builds to preserve the full benefit. They may restructure existing holdings to maximise the grandfathered advantages. They may use the carry-forward provisions strategically across financial years. The tactics change. The principle - that structure matters more than any single tax concession - does not.

The dual income couple remains the household best positioned to navigate these changes, because they have more structural levers to work with: two incomes, two marginal rates, two superannuation accounts, and the ability to allocate ownership and deductions across both partners in a way that responds to whatever the tax system does next.

But the real power of negative gearing - whether in its current form or its proposed future form - is not the deduction itself. It is what the deduction enables. The couple who directs their tax savings into an offset account is simultaneously reducing the interest on their home loan. The couple who uses the withholding variation to increase their fortnightly cash flow can accelerate their savings rate without earning a single additional dollar. The benefit is not static. It circulates. It compounds. Every dollar the tax system returns to a well-structured household is a dollar that starts working again immediately - against the mortgage, toward the next deposit, inside the superannuation contribution strategy. The structure does not just save money. It creates velocity.

This is why two couples with identical properties and identical incomes can arrive at entirely different financial positions after a decade. The bricks are the same. The structure around the bricks is not.

The tax system doesn't reward the highest earners. It rewards the best-structured households. And structure is a choice, not a salary.

What Rebecca and Lachlan Discovered

Back in Kellyville, the answer to Rebecca's question turned out to be exactly what she suspected - not that Olivia and Nav had a better accountant, but that they had a better structure.

Olivia and Nav had done two things that Rebecca and Lachlan had not:

1. They had kept their offset account linked to their home loan - the non-deductible debt - rather than parking it against the investment.
2. They had put a lot more of the loan in Nav's name than Olivia
3. They took out a higher loan amount on interest only than Rebecca and Lachlan

The property was nearly identical. The income was nearly identical. The structure was different. And the structure was worth almost $7,000 a year in total household benefit.

Rebecca called their bank the following week to move the offset. By the end of the next financial year, their position had shifted meaningfully. Lachlan, who had originally dismissed the gap as someone else's luck, put it more directly: 'Same bricks, different paperwork. That's all it was.'

That is all it ever is. The bricks don't change. The structure around them does. And in the Australian tax system - whether in its current form or the one taking shape in the 2026 Budget - that structure is worth more than most couples will ever realise, until someone shows them.

WEALTH BUILDER REFLECTION

One question to sit with:
If you mapped out how your investment property is financed - how much is deductible, how much is sitting in your offset, and whether the benefit is reaching you each fortnight or once a year - would the structure look like one that was designed, or one that just happened?

One truth to keep:
The tax system is not neutral. It is designed. And it is designed to reward the couple who understands the structure - not the couple who earns the most.

Chapter 7 crosses to the other side of the ledger. If property is the first engine, shares are the second - and for most Australian couples, they are the engine that has been sitting idle in the garage for years. It is time to start it.

PART THREE

Building Wealth with Shares

CHAPTER 7

Shares & ETFs

Systems beat single decisions

It's a Wednesday night in Caringbah, and Tom is sitting on the edge of the bathtub while Erin bathes their daughter. The bathroom is warm and loud - splashing, a rubber duck being interrogated, the extractor fan doing nothing useful. It is not the moment for a financial disclosure, which is probably why Tom chooses it.

'I bought some shares today,' he says.

Erin looks up from the bath. Her hands are wet. There is shampoo on her forearm. She has the expression of someone deciding whether to engage with this now or file it for later.

'Which ones?'

'Afterpay.'

She waits.

'A bloke at work's been in it for six months. He's up forty per cent. I put five grand in.'

Erin does not say what she is thinking, which is that five thousand dollars is exactly the amount they had set aside for the hot water system that has been making a sound neither of them wants to investigate. She asks a different question instead.

'Do you know what Afterpay actually does?'

Tom hesitates. 'It's a buy-now-pay-later thing. Tech. It's going up.'

Their daughter drops the duck. Nobody picks it up.

Three months later, the share price has dropped twenty-two per cent. Tom checks it every morning in the car park at work. He has not told Erin about the second time he checks, which is in the bathroom before bed. He is doing mental arithmetic at traffic lights. The hot water system has started making the sound more often.

Six months after that, he sells. The loss is not catastrophic - just over eleven hundred dollars, after brokerage. But the real cost is something the number cannot capture. It is the quiet conclusion Tom has drawn from the experience, one that millions of Australians draw every year:

Shares are gambling. Property is real. I'm not doing that again.

He is wrong. But not in the way he thinks.

Tom's mistake was not investing in shares. His mistake was making a single decision - one company, one tip, one moment of confidence borrowed from someone else - and calling it investing. He picked a stock the way you pick a horse: on a feeling, on a mate's conviction, with money budgeted for something else. That is not investing. That is speculation wearing investing's clothes.

And it is the reason most Australian couples never build the second engine at all.

The Myth

The problem is not that Australian couples avoid shares because they are unintelligent. They avoid shares because every experience they have had - or heard about - confirms the same story: someone bought a hot stock, it went up, it went down, they lost money, they felt sick. The conclusion is always the same. Shares are risky. Property is safe.

But this conclusion is built on a false comparison. They are comparing a single stock pick - concentrated, speculative, emotional - to an entire property market. They are comparing their worst day in one asset class to their best decade in another. And that lopsided comparison has been costing them quietly for years.

This chapter is about a different way into the share market. One that does not require stock picking, market timing, or financial expertise. One that is built on a system rather than a single decision. And one that, for the Australian dual-income couple, comes with a structural tax advantage most people have heard of, but almost nobody uses properly.

The share market is not a casino. But if you walk in with a single bet and no system, it will feel like one.

WEALTH BUILDERS THROUGH TIME

The Merchants Who Bought the Whole Market - Amsterdam, 1602–1700

In the early 1600s, the Dutch Republic was the commercial centre of the world. Amsterdam's harbour was the busiest in Europe, its banking system the most advanced, and its merchant class the wealthiest per capita on earth. It was here, in 1602, that something was invented that would reshape how ordinary people build wealth: the joint-stock company.

The Dutch East India Company - the Vereenigde Oost-Indische Compagnie, or VOC - was not the first business venture to sell shares. But it was the first to sell them to the general public, on an open exchange, with prices that moved daily based on supply and demand. For the first time in history, a merchant did not need to own a ship to profit from trade. He could own a piece of a system.

Most Amsterdam merchants in the early decades of the exchange behaved exactly the way Tom behaved in Caringbah four hundred years later. They picked individual ventures. They listened to tips at the coffee houses along the Damrak. They bought shares in specific voyages - this ship, that captain, this route to the Spice Islands - and waited to see whether the cargo returned or the ship sank. The returns, when they came, were spectacular. A single successful voyage could return three or four times the investment.

But the losses were equally spectacular. Ships were lost to storms, piracy, disease, and miscalculation. A merchant who concentrated his capital in a single venture could be wealthy in January and ruined by June. The exchange was exhilarating. It was also, for the concentrated speculator, frequently devastating.

A quieter kind of merchant emerged over the following decades - families who made a structural decision that their contemporaries found puzzling. Rather than selecting individual voyages, they spread their capital across many. They bought small positions in dozens of ventures, accepting that some would fail, some would break even, and a handful would return extraordinary profits. They did not try to pick the best ships. They bought the fleet.

The logic was not sophisticated. It was arithmetic. If one voyage in five sank, and the four that survived returned an average of sixty per cent, the merchant who held all five was ahead - consistently, reliably, without needing to predict which ship would go down. The merchant who picked the single voyage he believed in most had a one-in-five chance of losing everything.

This approach was mocked. The concentrated speculators called the diversified merchants timid. Unambitious. The coffee house wisdom was clear: real wealth came from conviction. From knowing which captain to trust, which route to back, which cargo would fetch the highest price in Batavia. Spreading your money across everything was an admission that you did not know enough to choose.

The diversified merchants did not argue. They simply kept buying the fleet.

By the mid-1600s, the pattern was undeniable. The concentrated speculators produced a handful of spectacular fortunes - and a far larger number of spectacular ruins. Families who had bet everything on the right ship one year would bet everything on the wrong ship the next. The famous Tulip Mania of 1637, in which speculative positions in tulip bulbs collapsed almost overnight, was merely the most visible example of a cycle that the concentrated merchants lived and died by: exhilarating rises, devastating falls, and the slow erosion of capital that comes from needing to be right every single time.

The diversified families produced something less dramatic and far more durable: steady, compounding wealth that grew across decades and survived every disruption the century threw at them - wars with England, trade route shifts, the Tulip crisis itself, and multiple corrections on the Amsterdam exchange. They did not need to be right about any single decision. They needed to be patient enough to let the system work.

And the system, given time, worked.

What the diversified Amsterdam merchants understood - perhaps before anyone else in history - was that a system of many small positions, held patiently, will outperform a series of single brilliant bets over any period long enough to matter. The individual voyage is unpredictable. The fleet is not.

The tools have changed. The principle hasn't.

An Australian couple in 2026 does not need to pick individual companies any more than a seventeenth-century Amsterdam merchant needed to pick individual ships. The vehicle exists that lets them buy the whole fleet - and it costs less than a cup of coffee a week to operate.

A PRESENT-DAY STORY

The Couple Who Stopped Picking and Started Building

Rachel and Dev came to see me in late 2018 with a problem that surprised them both. They were doing well - combined income around $290,000, a home in Epping with solid equity, one investment property in Wollongong that was performing steadily. They had been talking about shares for years. They had even opened a brokerage account eighteen months earlier with one of the major online platforms.

It was still empty. They just couldn't agree on how to invest.

Dev was an engineer by training and by temperament. He approached share investing the way he approached everything: he researched. He read annual reports. He built spreadsheets comparing price-to-earnings ratios across ASX-listed companies. He followed three finance podcasts and two YouTube channels. He had a shortlist of twelve companies he was 'almost ready' to buy.

He had been almost ready for a year and a half.

Rachel, who managed procurement for a private hospital group, had a simpler view. She wanted to put money into shares the way they put money into the mortgage: regularly, automatically, without having to think about it every fortnight. She did not want to become a share market expert. She wanted a system.

Dev thought Rachel's approach was reckless - throwing money at the market without understanding what you were buying. Rachel thought Dev's approach was a sophisticated form of procrastination - using research as an excuse to never actually act. They were both partially right. And they were stuck in the gap between those two positions, increasingly frustrated with each other, while the brokerage account sat at zero.

The more Dev researched, the more reasons he found not to act. Every company had risks he could identify. Every sector had headwinds he could name. The act of studying the market had made him more knowledgeable and less decisive simultaneously. He knew more than almost anyone he worked with about Australian equities. He owned none of them.

Rachel, meanwhile, had stopped raising the topic. She was tired of the same conversation ending the same way - Dev agreeing they should start, then finding one more thing to research before they did. She had started to wonder whether shares would happen at all.

The shift came in our meeting. I pulled up the ASX 200 index and showed them what had happened to it over the eighteen months since they had opened their brokerage account and done nothing. The index had returned just over six per cent in that period, including dividends. If they had put $100,000 in on the day they opened the account - which they could have comfortably done from their offset - it would have been worth roughly $106,000. Not from picking the right stocks or reading a single annual report. Just from owning the market and leaving it alone.

Dev went quiet. He had spent eighteen months researching which companies to buy. In that same eighteen months, the market itself - requiring no research, no decisions, no expertise - had generated six thousand dollars in returns that he and Rachel had simply not collected.

'Six thousand dollars,' Rachel said. 'For doing nothing.'

'For doing the right nothing,' I said.

That night, Rachel and Dev made a decision. They would invest in two exchange-traded funds: a Vanguard Australian Shares ETF tracking the ASX 300, giving them exposure to the entire Australian share market, and a Vanguard International Shares ETF tracking the world's largest companies outside Australia. Two funds. Two holdings. The whole fleet, in two purchases.

No individual stock picks. No sector bets. No timing. Just the system.

They set up an automatic transfer of $800 a fortnight from their transaction account. It came out on the same day as the mortgage. They treated it identically - a non-negotiable payment into their future, not a discretionary decision to be rethought every month.

It was Rachel's approach, built on the evidence Dev needed to trust it. For the first time in eighteen months, they were aligned.

The early months were harder for Dev than for Rachel. He watched the portfolio closely - something Rachel refused to do. When the market dipped seven per cent in late 2018, Dev spent an evening researching whether they should pause the contributions and wait for a better entry point.

Rachel asked him one question: 'Did you pause the mortgage payment?'

He hadn't.

'Then why would you pause this one?'

She was right, and the reason she was right goes to the heart of what makes systematic investing work. When you buy into a broad index at regular intervals, a falling market is not a threat. It is a sale. The same $800 buys more units when prices are low and fewer when prices are high. Over time, this mechanical process smooths out the volatility that terrifies the single-decision investor and turns it into an advantage for the systematic one.

Dev stopped checking daily. Then weekly. By the six-month mark, the portfolio had become what Rachel always wanted it to be: a system running quietly in the background, requiring nothing from either of them except the patience to leave it alone.

Then came March 2020. When COVID hit, and the ASX fell thirty-five per cent in five weeks, Dev rang me on a Tuesday morning. I could hear it in his voice - not panic exactly, but tightly controlled distress. He wanted to sell. Not all of it - just enough to 'protect what they had.'

I told him something I have said to more clients than I can count, and it is true every time: 'If we die, you don't need the money. And if we don't, you'll be a lot richer.'

He went home and told Rachel. She liked that. She laughed - the kind of laugh that reminds you that the world is not actually ending.

They kept the automatic investment running. They did not increase it. They did not decrease it. They changed nothing. The $800 went out every fortnight, buying more units of VAS and VGS than it had ever bought before, at prices they would never see again.

By December 2020, their portfolio had recovered fully and moved into profit. By mid-2021, the units they had purchased automatically during the crash - the ones bought in March, April, and May of 2020 - had individually gained more than sixty per cent. Not because they had timed the bottom. Because the system had bought through it.

Dev did the maths afterwards, because Dev always does the maths. If they had paused contributions for six months and resumed in September 2020, their portfolio would have been worth roughly $22,000 less by the end of 2021. *Twenty-two thousand dollars.* Not lost by a bad decision but by the absence of the system during the months it mattered most.

'I would have outsmarted myself,' he said. 'Rachel's system saved us twenty-two grand.'

It was the first time he had called it Rachel's system. She noticed.

Dev and Rachel did not need to become share market experts. They did not need to pick the right companies, time the right entry point, or predict a pandemic. They needed a system - one that removed the single decision from the process and replaced it with a mechanical, repeatable, emotionally neutral structure that worked whether they were paying attention or not.

The system does not care about headlines. It does not care about tips. It does not care about the bloke at work who is up forty per cent on something. It buys. It holds. It compounds. And over every period long enough to matter, it wins.

The share market doesn't reward the smartest investor. It rewards the most systematic one. And the system is available to every Australian couple willing to start it.

THE AUSTRALIAN APPLICATION

What an ETF Actually Is - And Why It Changes Everything

An exchange-traded fund is not complicated, despite what the financial industry has done to make it sound that way. It is a single investment that holds a basket of shares - dozens, hundreds, sometimes thousands of companies - in a single package. When you buy one unit of VAS, the Vanguard Australian Shares ETF, you own a small piece of every major company on the ASX. The big four banks. BHP. CSL. Woolworths. Wesfarmers. Three hundred companies, one purchase.

You do not need to research any of them individually. You do not need to decide which ones to include and which to leave out. You do not need to rebalance when one sector rises, and another falls. The ETF does all of this automatically, tracking the index it is designed to follow.

The cost is almost nothing. VAS charges a management fee of 0.07 per cent per year. On a $100,000 portfolio, that is $70 annually. A managed fund charging one per cent - which is modest by historical standards - would cost

$1,000 on the same amount. The difference in fees, compounded over twenty years, is significant enough to buy a decent second-hand car.

For the couple who has been standing at the edge of the share market, wanting to start but not sure where to step - this is the step. A broad Australian ETF like VAS or A200, paired with a global ETF like VGS, gives you the whole market. Not a bet on the market. The market itself.

How to Choose - And What to Ignore

Not all ETFs are created equal, and the financial industry has done a remarkable job of making a simple decision feel complicated. There are now hundreds of ETFs listed on the ASX - thematic funds, sector funds, leveraged funds, funds that track artificial intelligence companies, funds that track cryptocurrency miners, funds that track companies with high ESG scores. The choice appears overwhelming. It is not.

For the couple building a long-term wealth system, the selection criteria are short, and they have not changed in decades. You are looking for four things:

1. The first is breadth. You want an ETF that tracks a broad market index - not one that bets on a single sector or theme. A fund tracking artificial intelligence companies is not diversification. It is a concentrated bet dressed in an ETF wrapper. The whole point of the system is that you own the fleet, not a single ship. Breadth is how you do that.

   The simplest way to get breadth is to buy a single diversified ETF that holds everything - Australian shares, international shares, and sometimes bonds and property - inside one fund. Products like VDHG from Vanguard or DHHF from BetaShares do exactly this. One purchase. One holding. Automatic rebalancing between domestic and global markets without you needing to decide how much goes where. For the couple who wants the absolute simplest system - money in, leave it alone, let it compound - a single diversified ETF is the entire portfolio. You do not need to build anything more complicated than that unless you want to.

2. The second is cost. The management fee - sometimes called the MER, or management expense ratio - is the one variable entirely within your control. You cannot control what the market returns. But you can control how much of that return gets taken from you before it compounds. The fee is the leak in the bucket, and over time it is the difference between two portfolios that hold the same assets and produce very different outcomes. A broad index ETF should cost somewhere between 0.04 and 0.27 per cent per year. Anything above 0.30 per cent for a passive index fund is worth questioning. Anything above 0.50 per cent is a managed fund pretending to be an index fund. The difference between 0.07 per cent and 0.70 per cent, compounded over twenty years on a growing portfolio, is tens of thousands of dollars. It is the most expensive rounding error in personal finance.

3. The third is size. You want a fund with sufficient assets under management - generally above $500 million, and ideally above $1 billion. Larger funds have tighter tracking against their index, lower trading spreads, and a near-zero chance of being wound up by the provider. This is not a rule you need to research deeply. The major diversified ETFs from Vanguard, iShares, and BetaShares all clear this threshold comfortably.

4. The fourth is simplicity. If you cannot explain what the fund holds in one sentence - 'it owns a mix of every major company in Australia and around the world' - it is probably not the right fund for a long-term system. Complexity is not sophistication. In index investing, complexity is almost always cost in disguise.

What you can safely ignore is everything else. Past performance over the last one, three, or five years tells you almost nothing about the next one, three, or five. Star ratings from research houses reflect historical returns, not future ones. Thematic funds - technology, clean energy, ageing populations - require you to predict which theme will outperform, which is precisely the kind of single decision the system is designed to replace. And actively managed ETFs, which charge higher fees for the privilege of a fund manager picking stocks inside the wrapper, defeat the entire purpose of owning the index.

The choice, in practice, comes down to one or two funds from two or three providers. A single diversified ETF that holds Australian and international shares in one package. Or, if you want slightly more control, one Australian broad-market fund and one global fund. That is the decision. It takes an evening. It does not take eighteen months.

Understanding Risk - And What Time Does to It

Before a couple starts investing, they usually want to talk about risk. And the conversation almost always begins in the wrong place - because most people think of risk as a single thing. It is not. Risk is a scale, and where you sit on it depends almost entirely on one variable: time.

Think of it as a scale from one to ten. At one, you have cash in a bank account. It feels like the safest place in the world. And it nearly is - but even cash carries risk. Banks can fail. It has happened in Australia, though it is rare. Deposit guarantees cover the first $250,000 per institution. Beyond that, even the most conservative position is not perfectly safe. It is just very, very close to it.

At ten, you have a portfolio fully invested in shares. In any given month or quarter, it can fall significantly. Twenty per cent. Thirty per cent. In March

2020, it fell thirty-five per cent in five weeks. On the scale, a ten feels like the riskiest position you can take.

Here is what the scale does not tell you until you understand the role of time.

A 'scale-ten' held for three months is volatile. A 'scale-ten' held for three years is less so. A 'scale-ten' held for ten years - in a broadly diversified fund holding hundreds or thousands of companies across the Australian and global markets - has historically never produced a negative return over any rolling ten-year period on the ASX. Not once. Not through the GFC. Not through COVID. Not through any correction in between.

Time does not eliminate the risk. But it compresses it. It turns the sharp edges into gentle curves. A ten held long enough starts to feel like a one - not because the volatility disappears, but because the volatility stops mattering. The portfolio rises, falls, rises further, falls less, and over time the direction is unmistakable.

The couple who understands this makes a different decision from the couple who does not. The first couple sees a thirty per cent drop and thinks: the system is buying at thirty per cent off. The second couple sees the same drop and thinks: we are losing money. They are both looking at the same number. They are reading it through different timeframes.

This is why the system matters more than the selection. The right ETF held for eighteen months and then sold in a panic will underperform the wrong ETF held patiently for a decade. The risk is not in the product. It is in the behaviour. And behaviour, unlike markets, is something a couple *can* control.

The Advantage Most Australian Couples Leave on the Table

Here is where the Australian share market offers something that most couples have heard of but few have truly absorbed. It is called the *franking credit system*. For a dual-income household, it is one of the quietest, most powerful wealth-building advantages available anywhere in the world.

Here is how it works, in plain language. When an Australian company earns a profit, it pays company tax at 30 per cent before it distributes anything to shareholders. When that company then pays a dividend to you, the tax has already been paid. The dividend arrives with a credit attached - a franking credit - that tells the ATO: this income has already been taxed once at the company level. Do not tax it again at the full rate.

When you lodge your tax return, that franking credit is applied as a tax offset. If your marginal tax rate is higher than thirty per cent, you pay the difference. If your marginal rate is equal to or lower than thirty per cent - and this is where it gets interesting for dual income couples - the credit either covers the tax exactly or the excess comes back to you as a refund.

Consider a practical example, using the current tax rates at the time of writing. An Australian company pays you a fully franked dividend of $700. The franking credit attached to that dividend is $300 - representing the company tax already paid. Your taxable income for that dividend is $1,000 ($700 cash plus $300 credit). If your marginal rate is 30 per cent - the rate that currently applies to taxable income between $45,001 and $135,000 - your tax on that $1,000 is $300. The franking credit covers it exactly. You owe no additional tax on the $700 of dividend income. It is a clean offset.

If your marginal rate is lower - say 16 cents in the dollar, which currently applies to taxable income between $18,201 and $45,000 - the credit exceeds your tax liability and the ATO refunds the difference. The company has already paid thirty cents in the dollar. You only owe sixteen. The other fourteen cents comes back to you.

Now here is the part that you might not expect.

In a dual income household where one partner earns significantly more than the other - perhaps because one has reduced hours for family, or works in a lower-paying profession - the franking credits work harder when the dividends flow through the lower earner's name. The same dividend, from the same company, in the same household, produces a different tax outcome depending on which partner holds it. This is not a loophole. It is the design of the system. The Australian imputation system was introduced in 1987 precisely to prevent the double taxation of company profits. It rewards the Australian shareholder. It rewards the couple who holds shares in a tax-aware structure. And it compounds alongside the capital growth of the shares themselves, creating two parallel engines of return - growth and income - inside a single investment.

The Australian share market has historically paid dividend yields of four to five per cent, among the highest of any developed market in the world. Those dividends, franked at thirty per cent, flowing into the right structure within a dual income household, create a compounding tax advantage that grows every year. Most couples either do not know about franking credits, or they know the name without understanding the mechanics. The couple who understands the mechanics makes different decisions - about which partner holds the shares, about whether to reinvest dividends or redirect them into an offset account, about how the share portfolio interacts with the rest of their tax position. Those decisions, individually small, compound into an advantage that is difficult to replicate through any other means.

These tax rates may change - they have been adjusted several times in recent years, and further reductions to the lower brackets are already legislated. But the franking credit system itself has been a structural feature of Australian taxation since 1987, and the principle behind it has not changed: the couple who holds Australian shares in a considered structure pays less tax than the couple who doesn't.

The Australian share market doesn't just pay you to invest. It pays you in a way that the tax system was specifically designed to reward. The couple who understands this has an engine most of the world doesn't.

The System in Practice

What does systematic share investing actually look like inside a dual-income Australian household? It looks unremarkable; that is the point.

A couple opens a brokerage account - through one of the low-cost Australian platforms like CommSec, SelfWealth, or Stake. They choose one or two broad index ETFs - or a single diversified fund that holds everything in one package. They set up a regular automatic transfer, fortnightly or monthly, in an amount that is meaningful but not painful. Three hundred dollars. Five hundred. Eight hundred. Whatever the household can sustain without disrupting the mortgage payments, the offset strategy, or the cost of running a family.

The transfer is automatic. It is not a decision that gets made fresh each pay cycle. It is a standing instruction, identical in function to the mortgage repayment. Money moves from the transaction account into the brokerage account without anyone needing to approve it, think about it, or feel good about the market that week.

When the market rises, the automatic investment buys fewer units. When the market falls, it buys more. Over time, this mechanical process produces an average entry price that is lower than the average market price - not by a dramatic margin, but by enough to matter across a decade of compounding.

Dividends are either reinvested automatically - buying more units without any action required - or directed into an offset account, where they reduce mortgage interest while remaining accessible. Both strategies are valid. The right choice depends on the household's broader structure, not on a general rule.

The couple does not watch the market daily. They do not react to headlines. They do not sell when the market drops and they do not buy extra when it surges. They run the system. The system runs itself.

This is not exciting. It is not meant to be. The most powerful wealth-building strategies rarely are. The mortgage is not exciting. The superannuation contribution is not exciting. The automatic share investment is the third pillar of the same quiet, compounding architecture - and for most Australian couples, it is the pillar they have never built.

What Tom and Erin Did Differently the Second Time

Eighteen months after Tom sold his Afterpay shares at a loss, Erin came across an article that described index investing in language she understood. No jargon. No stock picks. Just the idea that you could own the entire Australian share market through a single ETF for less than a dollar a week in fees, and that doing so had historically outperformed the vast majority of people who tried to be clever about it.

She showed it to Tom over dinner. He was resistant. The scar tissue from the Afterpay experiment was still fresh. Shares meant risk. Shares meant checking your phone in the car park. Shares meant the hot water system they had put on the credit card.

But Erin's proposal was different from what Tom had done. She did not want to pick stocks or follow tips. She wanted to set up an automatic investment of $400 a fortnight into VAS - the Vanguard Australian Shares ETF - and forget about it.

'No checking it,' she said. 'No changing it. It goes out like the mortgage. We look at it once a year, at tax time, and that's it.'

Tom agreed, reluctantly.

Twelve months later, he was no longer reluctant. The portfolio had grown - not dramatically, but steadily, in a way that felt entirely different from the Afterpay experience. There had been no single moment of exhilaration and no single moment of dread—just a quiet, accumulating number that moved in one direction more often than the other.

The dividends, fully franked, had arrived in their account twice that year. When their accountant lodged the returns, the franking credits offset a small portion of their tax bill - not a transformative amount in the first year, but real money back from the ATO that they would not have received if the portfolio had not existed. The system was not just growing. It was working inside their broader tax position, quietly, in ways that a single stock pick never could. And the offset would grow every year as the portfolio grew beneath it.

Tom said something over dinner one night that told me the shift was real: 'Afterpay felt like gambling. This feels like building. I don't know why I thought they were the same thing.'

They are not the same thing. And the difference is not the asset. It is the approach. A single decision is a bet. A system is a structure. The bet depends on being right. The structure depends only on being patient.

WEALTH BUILDER REFLECTION

One question to sit with:
What has been stopping us from starting the second engine - and is the reason we've been giving ourselves *actually* a reason, or is it the echo of someone else's bad experience?

One truth to keep:
You don't need to pick the right shares. You need to build the right system. The market rewards the couple who shows up consistently far more than it rewards the one who shows up brilliantly.

Chapter 8 asks the question that every couple faces once the system is running: what happens when the market falls, the headlines scream, and every instinct says to stop the automatic transfer? The answer is not courage. It is something quieter, learnable, and far more useful - and it is the skill that separates the couple who builds wealth from the couple who merely tries to.

CHAPTER 8

How to Invest Without the Stress

Emotional regulation is a wealth skill.

It is a Tuesday night in Parramatta, and Jen is standing in the kitchen doorway watching her husband do something she has asked him three times to stop doing.

Ravi is sitting at the dining table with his phone in one hand and a calculator app open on his laptop. He has been there for forty minutes. The remains of dinner are still on the bench. The kids have put themselves to bed, which at seven and nine is not a good sign because he usually reads to them before bed.

'How much are we down?' Jen asks. Ravi looks at her with a downtrodden expression that already gives enough of an answer. 'The property is worth less than we paid for it,' Ravi says. 'If we sold right now, we'd lose sixty grand. And the shares are down fourteen per cent since January.'

It is May 2022. The Reserve Bank has just raised the cash rate for the first time in over a decade. The financial press is using phrases like: *correction*, *headwinds* and *pain ahead*. Every headline Ravi reads confirms what his body has been telling him for weeks: *something is wrong, and they need to do something about it before it gets worse.*

Jen sits down across from him. She does not look at the screen.

'What do you want to do?' she asks.

'Sell the investment property. Pause the share contributions. Put everything into the offset and wait until this is over.'

He says it with the certainty of someone who has been rehearsing the sentence in his head all evening. Jen recognises the tone. It is the same tone he used when he wanted to walk the kids to school instead of drive because petrol prices went up. It is the voice of a man who is not making a financial decision. He is making an emotional one.

She does not say this. She says: 'Let's not decide anything tonight.'

Ravi exhales. He does not agree. But he does not argue. They go to bed without resolving anything, which feels like failure to Ravi and feels like the only sane option to Jen.

What neither of them knows yet - what they will only understand eighteen months later, looking back - is that the most valuable financial skill they will ever develop is not picking the right investment; it is learning not to act on a feeling that mistakes the last three months for the next ten years.

The market doesn't test your intelligence. It tests your nervous system. And most couples have never trained for that.

This chapter is not about what to invest in; the earlier chapters have covered that ground. This chapter is about what happens inside you after you have invested - and why that matters more than almost anything else in determining your outcome.

The financial industry spends an extraordinary amount of energy helping people choose investments and almost no energy helping them hold them. This is like teaching someone to plant a garden and then never mentioning that there will be storms. Planting is the easy part. Holding is where the wealth is made or lost.

Every couple who builds a portfolio of property and shares will, at some point, face a moment like the one Ravi and Jen did at their dining table. The market will fall. The headlines will scream. The mortgage payments will rise. And in that moment, the question is not what the market is doing. *The question is what they are doing.*

The couples who sell at the bottom are not making a financial decision. They are making a psychological one. Their nervous system has interpreted a temporary decline as a permanent threat, and it is demanding action. Any action. The kind of action that feels like control but is, in almost every measurable case, the most expensive thing they could do.

The couples who hold - who change nothing, who let the system run, who endure the discomfort of watching numbers fall without reaching for the phone - are not braver. They are not smarter. They have something the others don't: a structure that makes stillness possible when everything inside them is screaming to move.

WEALTH BUILDERS THROUGH TIME

The Day Melbourne's Nerves Were Tested - October 1987

On Tuesday, 20 October 1987, the Australian share market opened to something no one alive had ever seen. The All Ordinaries index (a giant scoreboard that counts the points of the 500 biggest companies in Australia to show if all the companies are winning or losing together over a certain period) fell 25 per cent in a single day. By the end of the week, it had lost more than a third of its value. By the time the selling exhausted itself, the market had fallen nearly 50 per cent from its September peak. Fortunes built across decades evaporated in weeks.

Melbourne, which had been riding a wave of post-deregulation prosperity, was at the centre of the wreckage. The city's business families - manufacturers, importers, retail operators, property developers - held significant share portfolios alongside their operating businesses and their property. Many had leveraged against those portfolios to fund expansion. The crash did not merely reduce their wealth on paper. It called in their debts.

Two kinds of families existed in Melbourne that October. The distinction between them had been invisible during the boom. It became the only thing that mattered during the crash.

The first kind had built their position on momentum. They had borrowed against rising share prices to fund further purchases. Their property holdings were leveraged to finance share investments, and their share portfolios were leveraged to finance property. Every asset was connected to every other asset through a web of debt that worked beautifully in a rising market and catastrophically in a falling one.

The second kind had built their position on structure. They held shares and property, but they also held something their leveraged neighbours considered wasteful: cash. Reserves. Money sitting in bank accounts doing nothing except reducing their exposure to exactly this kind of moment. Their friends had teased them about it during the boom years. Why hold cash when the market returns twelve per cent? Why leave money idle when it could be working?

When the crash came, the leveraged families faced margin calls they could not meet. Their brokers demanded additional security. Their banks demanded repayments. The only way to meet those demands was to sell - and selling into a market that was falling twenty per cent a week meant crystallising losses at the worst possible prices. The act of selling, which felt like the only option, was the thing that turned a temporary crisis into a permanent one.

The families with reserves did something that looked, to everyone around them, like either courage or madness. They held. Some of them bought. They endured weeks of falling prices, months of uncertainty, and the quiet social pressure of being the family that hadn't sold when the newspapers said selling was the only rational response.

They did not hold because they were certain the market would recover. They held because their structure allowed them to. They had no margin calls. They had no debt demanding immediate repayment. They had the one thing the leveraged families lacked: time.

Within two years, the All Ordinaries had recovered the majority of its losses. Within five, it had surpassed its pre-crash peak. The families who had held through the worst of it emerged with portfolios that were now growing from a base they had never been forced to sell. The families who had been forced to sell were still rebuilding - or gone entirely.

The 1987 crash did not sort Melbourne's investors by intelligence, conviction, or courage. It sorted them by structure. The families with reserves could regulate their response because their finances did not demand panic. The families without reserves could not regulate their response because their finances were the source of the panic.

Emotional regulation was not a personality trait those families possessed. It was a structural outcome their reserves produced.

The tools have changed. The principle hasn't.

An Australian couple in 2026 will never face the exact conditions of October 1987. But they will face rate cycles, corrections, and the relentless noise of a financial media designed to provoke exactly the kind of reaction Ravi had at his dining table. The question is not whether the storm will come. It is whether their structure can survive it.

A PRESENT-DAY STORY

The Couple Who Built a Buffer and Then Forgot About It

Sophie and Marco came to see me in early 2021. Sophie was a physiotherapist running her own practice in Cronulla. Marco was a project manager for a mid-size construction firm in the Shire. Combined income around $240,000. They owned their home in Miranda with a mortgage of $920,000, and they had just settled on their first investment property - a two-bedroom unit in Hurstville that had cost them $780,000.

They had also, six months earlier, started a modest share portfolio. Four hundred dollars a fortnight into an ASX 200 ETF, set up on autopilot. Between the investment property and the shares, they were running both engines for the first time. They were proud of it, and they should have been.

But there was a gap in their structure that neither of them could see yet. Their offset account against the home loan held about $35,000. Their emergency savings sat in a separate high-interest account with $8,000. Against nearly $1.7 million in combined mortgage debt, they had less than four weeks of buffer.

I told them this was the one thing I wanted them to fix before they did anything else; before they increased the share contributions, before they thought about a second investment property... Before any of it.

'Build the offset to six to twelve months of your home loan payments and living costs,' I said. 'Not because you'll need it financially. Because you'll need it psychologically.'

We settled on nine months. Rates were low, the economy was stable, and nine months of their home loan and living costs came to just over ninety thousand dollars. It felt like a lot of money to park. It was.

Marco looked sceptical. 'Ninety grand sitting there doing nothing.'

'It's not doing nothing. It's reducing your mortgage interest every single day. And it's buying you the ability to make no decision at all during the next downturn.'

They didn't fully understand what I meant. *Not yet.*

Over the following twelve months, Sophie and Marco redirected every spare dollar into the offset account. They paused the share contributions temporarily - something I rarely suggest, but in this case the buffer mattered more than three quarters of additional compounding. Marco picked up a short-term contract on weekends. Sophie's practice had a strong quarter. By February 2022, the offset held $92,000.

They resumed the share contributions. The offset sat there, reducing their home loan interest by roughly $370 a month, doing its quiet financial work. But its real job - the one that would justify every dollar and every weekend Marco worked - was about to begin.

In May 2022, the Reserve Bank raised the cash rate for the first time in eleven years. Then again in June. And again in July. By the time the cycle paused eighteen months later, the cash rate had moved from 0.10 per cent to 4.35 per cent - the fastest tightening cycle in a generation.

The effect on Sophie and Marco's cash flow was immediate and painful. Their home loan repayments increased by over $2,200 a month. The investment property, which had been mildly positively geared at the old rate, swung to a loss of $480 a week. Their share portfolio dropped sixteen per cent in 3 months.

Every number on every screen was moving in the wrong direction. And every conversation they had with friends and colleagues confirmed the same narrative: *things are bad, they're getting worse, and anyone still holding is taking a risk they don't need to take.*

Marco wanted to sell the Hurstville unit. The property was costing them money every week. If rates kept rising, the loss would deepen. They could sell, clear the investment mortgage, and wait. It felt like the responsible thing to do.

Sophie listened. Then she asked a question that changed the conversation.

'Can we survive twelve more months without selling?'

Marco looked at the offset account. Ninety-two thousand dollars. Even with the higher repayments, even with the property running at a loss, even with the increased cost of everything else - they could cover the gap for at least ten months without touching anything. Twelve, if they trimmed a few discretionary expenses.

'Yes,' he said. 'But -'

'Then we don't sell.'

It was not a financial argument. It was a structural one. The offset account - the buffer Marco had once called ninety grand doing nothing - was doing the most important thing it would ever do. It was giving them permission to sit still.

Without the buffer, the conversation would have been different. Without nine months of runway, the rising costs would have forced a decision. Not because selling was the right move, but because their structure would have demanded it. They would have been the 1987 leveraged family, selling at the bottom, not out of strategy but out of structural necessity. The offset was the difference between a choice and a compulsion.

They held. They did not enjoy it. Marco checked the property's estimated value weekly for the first three months, then fortnightly, then not at all. Sophie stopped reading the finance pages entirely. They made small adjustments - cancelled a streaming service, ate out less, deferred a holiday - but they changed nothing structural. The mortgage payments went out. The share contributions went out. The investment property sat there, doing what investment properties do during a rate cycle.

By mid-2024, the picture had shifted. The Hurstville property, which Marco had wanted to sell for an estimated $720,000 in the depths of the downturn, was now valued at $880,000. The capital growth alone - the growth they would have forfeited by selling - was worth more than the total cost of holding through the rate cycle.

Their share portfolio had recovered and then some. The units purchased automatically during the downturn were individually up more than thirty per cent. The dividends, fully franked, had continued arriving throughout the correction.

The offset account, which had been drawn down to $58,000 during the worst months, had been rebuilt to $74,000 as rates stabilised and Sophie's practice grew. It had done its job, and it was refilling itself.

I sat down with them in late 2024 and ran the numbers on what would have happened if they had followed Marco's instinct in mid-2022 - sold the investment property, paused the shares, retreated to cash.

The difference was $243,000.

Not over a lifetime. Over two years. Two hundred and forty-three thousand dollars, lost not to a bad investment but to a decision made from panic—a decision the offset account had given them the structural ability to avoid.

Marco said something I hear more often than you might expect from clients who have just been shown what their worst instinct would have cost them.

'I wasn't wrong to be scared. I was wrong to think that being scared meant I had to do something.'

Sophie and Marco did not succeed because they were emotionally disciplined people. They are not. Marco will be the first to tell you that. They succeeded because they had built a structure that made emotional discipline unnecessary. The offset account did not change how they felt during the downturn. It changed what they needed to do about how they felt. And the difference between feeling panic and acting on panic is, over a decade of investing, the difference between building wealth and destroying it.

THE AUSTRALIAN APPLICATION

The Tool That Turns Fear Into Patience

In Chapter 4, the offset account was a structural tool - the holding bay that kept Mei and Chris' non-deductible interest low while their investment debt did the heavy lifting. That is what it does to a loan balance. It is not what it does to a couple.

Sophie and Marco did not hold through 2022 because they understood the mechanics. They understood them perfectly well in 2021, when the offset was just an account with money in it. What changed in the middle of a correction was what those two numbers - the balance and the months of runway it represented - did to the conversation they were able to have with each other. The offset had quietly stopped being a tax structure and become something else entirely.

The financial benefit is well understood by most people who have a mortgage. What is less well understood - and what matters far more for the long-term wealth builder - is the behavioural benefit.

A well-funded offset account changes the internal conversation during a downturn. When rates rise, when property values dip, when the share portfolio drops 15 per cent in a quarter, the couple with six to twelve months of expenses in the offset has a fundamentally different experience from the couple with three weeks. Not because the market is treating them differently. Because their nervous system is.

The couple with no buffer feels every rate rise as an existential threat. Their decision-making narrows. Their time horizon shrinks. They begin thinking in weeks instead of years. And decisions made in weeks instead of years are almost always the wrong ones. The couple with a funded offset feels the same discomfort, but the fear does not reach the threshold where it demands action. They can sit with it. They can let the market do what markets have always done - fall and then recover - without being forced to act during the falling.

This is observable in every rate cycle and every correction the Australian market has produced. The couples who hold through volatility and emerge wealthier are not the ones with the strongest nerves. They are the ones with the deepest buffers. The buffer does the work that willpower cannot.

How Much Is Enough?

The standard advice is three to six months of expenses in a buffer. That is sensible for a household with a single mortgage and no investment exposure. But a couple running the strategy in this book is likely carrying more moving parts than a standard household. When a rate cycle hits, you need enough runway to keep the household running and the investment engines fed without being forced to sell. For a couple building across both property and shares, the number is six to twelve months.

The calculation is simpler than most people expect: your home loan repayments and your core living costs - insurance, utilities, food, transport, school fees, the actual cost of running your household. The investment property is not included. It services itself through rent. What you are protecting is your ability to hold during the months when the numbers are at their lowest, without the household itself coming under enough pressure that it forces a sale.

Six months is the floor - the point at which most couples stop making fear-based decisions because the runway is long enough to survive the worst of a correction. Twelve months is where the system becomes genuinely stress-resistant: long enough to ride out a full rate cycle and keep the share contributions running through a downturn without touching the structure.

Yes, that money could be invested elsewhere. Yes, in a rising market, it might feel like dead capital. But it is not dead. It is reducing your mortgage interest every day, and it is performing the single most valuable function any dollar in your household can perform: it is keeping you in the game during the moments when the game gets hard.

The offset account isn't just a financial tool. It's a permission slip to do nothing when doing nothing is the hardest and most profitable thing you can do.

The Three Reactions That Cost Australian Couples the Most

Every downturn produces the same three mistakes:

1. Selling the investment property during a soft market - which crystallises a loss that was, until that moment, temporary.
2. Pausing the share contributions - which feels minor but means every dollar misses the recovery, the mathematical equivalent of leaving a sale because the discounts made you nervous.
3. Moving to cash entirely - which locks in losses and then introduces a second, often insurmountable problem: when do you get back in? The couple who moved to cash in March 2020 and waited for certainty before reinvesting missed one of the fastest recoveries in market history. By the time things felt safe, the market had already recovered and moved beyond them.

All three mistakes share a common root. They are not failures of intelligence; they are failures of structure. Fix the structure, and the mistakes become avoidable.

What Emotional Regulation Actually Looks Like

It does not look like confidence or calm. It does not look like two people sitting serenely at the dining table while the market burns around them.

It looks like Jen, standing in the kitchen doorway, watching her husband spiral, and saying: *Let's not decide anything tonight.*

It looks like Marco, staring at the offset account balance and realising that the answer to *can we survive this?* is *yes* - and that the answer is the only thing that matters.

It looks like a couple who has agreed, in advance, on one rule: no financial decisions during the first seventy-two hours of any market event. Not because seventy-two hours will fix anything. Because seventy-two hours is long enough for the nervous system to step back from the ledge and for the couple to talk about what is actually happening rather than what it feels like is happening.

The fear is real. The discomfort of watching your net worth decline on a screen is real. Emotional regulation is not the absence of those feelings. It is the presence of a structure that prevents those feelings from becoming decisions. The buffer in the offset. The automatic share contribution that runs whether you feel good about the market or not. The investment property with a lease that generates income regardless of what the valuation says this quarter. These are not financial products. They are emotional architecture.

The couple who can sit still during a storm will always finish ahead of the couple who runs. Not because sitting still is brave. Because running, in a market that always recovers, is the only way to make a temporary loss permanent.

WEALTH BUILDER REFLECTION

One question to sit with:

When was the last time we made a financial decision from calm - and when was the last time we made one from fear? What did each one cost us?

One truth to keep:
Emotional regulation is not a feeling you summon. It is a structure you build. The couple with six months in the offset and a system that runs on autopilot does not need courage during a downturn. They need patience. And patience, unlike courage, can be engineered.

Chapter 9 asks the question that most Australian couples have been told to avoid: can you use debt to invest in shares? The answer is yes - but only if you understand the structure that makes it safe, and the line between leverage and recklessness. It is a shorter walk than most people think.

CHAPTER 9

Using Debt to Invest in Shares

Optionality is power

It is a Saturday morning in Baulkham Hills, and Craig is reading something on his phone that is making him unusually quiet.

Tess notices from the kitchen. Craig is not a quiet person. He talks through breakfast, talks through the drive to Bunnings, talks through the walk around the block with the dog. Silence from Craig means he is either angry or thinking hard, and she has learned to tell the difference by the angle of his jaw.

He is thinking hard.

'What if we're doing the mortgage wrong?' he says, not looking up.

Tess puts down the kettle. They have been together for thirteen years. In that time, the mortgage has been the one thing they have never disagreed about. Pay it down. Pay it fast. Every spare dollar into the offset, every bonus against the principal. They are eighteen months ahead on their repayment schedule, and both of them are proud of it.

'What do you mean, wrong?'

'I mean - what if paying it off as fast as possible isn't actually the smartest move? What if there's a way to use the equity we've built to start investing in shares, and make the interest tax-deductible at the same time?'

Tess stares at him. She heard two things in that sentence. *Borrowing to invest in shares* and *tax-deductible*. The first one terrifies her. The second one sounds like something a bloke at a barbecue says right before explaining a scheme that loses everyone money.

'That sounds like leverage,' she says. 'People lose their houses doing that.'

Craig doesn't argue. He puts the phone down. But the question he has just asked - quietly, carefully, the way he always raises ideas he knows Tess will resist - is one that sits between them for the rest of the weekend. It sits there because Tess can't quite dismiss it. Because they borrowed $680,000 to buy their home without hesitation. They borrowed $520,000 for their investment property in Penrith without losing a night's sleep. But the idea of borrowing $50,000 to invest in a diversified share portfolio makes her feel physically uncomfortable.

She can't explain why. And that - the inability to explain why - is the thing that won't let her put it down.

You will borrow half a million dollars for a house you cannot sell quickly, in a market you cannot control, and call it responsible. But borrowing a fraction of that for a liquid, diversified portfolio you can exit in forty-eight hours feels reckless. The inconsistency is not yours. It is cultural. And it is costing you.

The Myth

This chapter asks Australian couples to sit with a discomfort most of them have never examined: the asymmetry between how they think about property debt and how they think about investment debt in shares.

If you are reading this book, it is likely you have taken on property debt or are planning to in the future. You understand leverage in the context of bricks and land. You accept that borrowing to buy an asset that grows over time is not reckless - it is how wealth is built. Their parents or friends most likely did it. The bank approved it. It feels normal.

But the same logic, applied to shares, triggers something different. Not a reasoned objection; a visceral one. Shares are volatile. Shares can go to zero. Shares are not real in the way a house is real. The idea of owing money on something you cannot see or touch feels fundamentally different from owing money on something with a roof and a front door.

This chapter does not ask you to become comfortable with reckless leverage. It asks you to understand that there is a structured, disciplined way to use debt to build a share portfolio - one that Australian couples are uniquely positioned to benefit from. This chapter asks you to understand the difference between leverage and recklessness is not the asset. It is the structure around it.

The principle is the same one that runs through every story of wealth built across generations: *optionality is power.* The couple who can deploy capital into shares when prices fall, who can convert dead equity into a working portfolio, who can restructure their debt from passive to active - that couple has options the mortgage-only household does not. And options, held patiently, are how ordinary wealth becomes extraordinary.

WEALTH BUILDERS THROUGH TIME

The Trust Builders of Dundee - Scotland, 1870–1910

In the early 1870s, the city of Dundee sat at the industrial heart of eastern Scotland. It was a city of jute mills and shipyards, where merchant families had accumulated capital through textile manufacturing and overseas trade. But by the 1870s, these families faced a problem that would be familiar to any modern Australian couple sitting on equity in a home: they had wealth locked inside their existing enterprises, and no obvious way to put it to work beyond the industries they already knew.

The local opportunities were narrowing. Jute margins were compressing. Shipping was consolidating into fewer, larger firms. The merchant families of Dundee had capital and ambition, but limited optionality - their money was trapped in a single market, a single country, a single industrial cycle.

Across the Atlantic, something entirely different was happening. The United States was laying thousands of miles of railway, opening farmland across the

Midwest, and issuing bonds and securities at yields that dwarfed anything available in Britain. The returns were real. But so were the risks. An individual Scottish merchant investing directly in an American railroad had almost no way to assess the creditworthiness of the issuer, no legal recourse if things went wrong, and no ability to diversify across enough ventures to absorb the inevitable failures.

The problem was not a lack of opportunity. It was a lack of a clear plan.

A group of Dundee merchants-led by a young clerk named Robert Fleming, who would later found the merchant bank that still bears his family name - held a belief that separated them from the cautious majority. They believed that leverage, applied to a diversified portfolio of securities rather than a single venture, was not reckless. It was rational. The key was the structure.

Their reasoning was precise. A single leveraged bet on one American railroad was speculation. But a trust that pooled capital from many investors, borrowed additional funds at low British interest rates, and spread the total across dozens of American securities was something fundamentally different. The diversification absorbed the individual failures. The leverage amplified the portfolio returns. And the spread between cheap British borrowing and high American yields created a structural margin of safety that no single investment could provide.

In 1873, Fleming helped establish the Scottish American Investment Trust - one of the first investment trusts in the world. The plan was elegant. Investors contributed capital. The trust then borrowed additional funds - typically between thirty and fifty per cent of the invested capital - and deployed the combined pool across a diversified portfolio of American bonds, railroad securities, and land mortgage investments.

The borrowed money was not speculative margin. It was structural leverage, governed by strict rules: maximum borrowing ratios, mandatory diversification across sectors and issuers, regular income requirements from underlying holdings, and clear covenants that prevented concentration in any single name. The trust could not bet everything on one railroad. It had to own the system.

Within a decade, similar trusts had been established across Edinburgh, Dundee, Glasgow, and London. The model spread because it worked - not in one cycle, but consistently, across varying market conditions.

The Scottish trusts were not universally admired. Conservative investors in London viewed them with deep suspicion. Borrowing to invest in securities was, in the gentlemen's clubs of the City, considered ungentlemanly at best and dangerous at worst. The same men who routinely borrowed against land and property to fund further acquisitions saw no parallel in borrowing against a portfolio of income-producing securities.

The criticism intensified during the Baring Crisis of 1890, when a major London bank nearly collapsed under the weight of Argentine bond losses. Several poorly managed trusts - those that had abandoned diversification rules and concentrated heavily in South American debt-failed alongside it. The critics pointed to these failures as proof that leveraged securities investing was inherently unsound.

But the well-structured Scottish trusts survived. Fleming's trust, and others that had maintained their diversification covenants and borrowing limits, weathered the crisis with their capital and income largely intact. The difference was not the use of leverage. It was the presence or absence of structural discipline around it.

By the early 1900s, the Scottish investment trust model had proven itself across three decades of market cycles, including a major financial crisis. The merchant families who had invested through these trusts had transformed locked-up industrial capital into diversified, income-producing portfolios that compounded quietly across generations.

Fleming himself went on to found the merchant bank Robert Fleming & Co., which managed wealth for families across the world for over a century. His grandson, Ian Fleming, would become better known for creating James Bond-a career made possible, in part, by the intergenerational wealth his grandfather had built through structured, leveraged investing in diversified securities.

The trusts that failed were the ones that treated leverage as a way to amplify conviction - borrowing more to bet more on a single outcome. The trusts that endured were the ones that treated leverage as a way to amplify a system - borrowing carefully to widen their exposure across many outcomes, with rules that prevented emotion from overriding the plan.

The Dundee merchants understood something that most investors, then and now, get backwards. Leverage is not inherently dangerous. Concentrated leverage is dangerous. Leverage applied to a diversified, income-producing portfolio, with structural limits on borrowing and mandatory rules that prevent deviation - that is not gambling. It is architecture.

And the families who built that architecture did not just protect their capital. They multiplied their options. They could invest in markets they could not otherwise access. They could compound returns they could not otherwise achieve. They had created something more valuable than a high return: they had created *optionality* - the ability to act when others could not, hold when others would not, and benefit from opportunities that were inaccessible to the unleveraged investor.

The tools have changed. The principle hasn't.

An Australian couple in 2026 does not need to form a trust in Dundee or navigate American railroad bonds. But the structural insight is identical. Debt, used with discipline and deployed into a diversified portfolio, is not the enemy. It is one of the most powerful tools available to the couple willing to build the plan around it.

A PRESENT-DAY STORY

The Couple Who Turned Dead Equity Into a Working Portfolio

Craig and Tess - the couple from Baulkham Hills - came in for a full review in early 2023. Craig was a logistics manager earning $125,000. Tess worked three days a week in dental practice management, earning $68,000. Combined income was just over $193,000. They owned their home, purchased eight years earlier for $780,000, now valued at roughly $1.05 million. The mortgage sat at $410,000. They also held an investment property in Penrith worth approximately $640,000, with a loan of $480,000.

On paper, they were in a strong position. Their home equity alone was over $640,000. But almost none of it was working for them.

The house would grow at whatever rate the market delivered, regardless of whether it carried a $410,000 mortgage or a $200,000 one. The equity did not accelerate the growth. It simply sat there - passive, silent, and entirely outside the tax system.

They had no share portfolio. Their superannuation balances-Craig's at $142,000 and Tess's at $87,000-had been untouched since they defaulted into their employer funds years ago.

They were ahead of schedule on the mortgage. They were disciplined savers. And they were quietly leaving hundreds of thousands of dollars of long-term wealth on the table because their only strategy was to pay down non-deductible debt as fast as possible.

Craig and Tess believed what most Australian couples believe: that the mortgage is the enemy, and the fastest path to financial freedom is killing it. Every financial conversation they'd had with family and friends reinforced this. Tess's parents had paid off their home by fifty and considered it the proudest financial achievement of their lives. Craig's mates at work talked about extra repayments the way athletes talk about personal bests.

The belief was not wrong. Paying down a home loan is never a bad decision. But it was incomplete - because it treated all debt as identical and all equity as inert. Their home loan interest was not tax-deductible. Every dollar of extra repayment reduced a liability, but it also locked capital inside an asset that would grow at the same rate regardless of how much they owed on it.

Craig's question on that Saturday morning - *what if we're doing the mortgage wrong?* - was the first crack in a belief that had been governing every financial decision they'd made as a couple.

Over three meetings, we built a debt recycling strategy. The concept is simple, though the mechanics require precision. Craig and Tess would draw down $120,000 from the available equity in their home loan and invest it into a diversified portfolio of income-producing Australian and international shares and ETFs. This was additional debt - their total borrowings would increase from $890,000 to $1,010,000. That is a fact, and it needs to be understood clearly before anything else.

But the nature of the new debt was fundamentally different from the old. Because the borrowed funds were used to produce assessable income-dividends from the share portfolio - the interest on the new $120,000 became tax-deductible. The non-deductible home loan balance remained at $410,000. Sitting alongside it was now $120,000 of deductible investment debt. The total was higher. The structure was categorically different.

The share portfolio was deliberately constructed for income and diversification. Australian ETFs provided franked dividend income. International ETFs provided exposure to global markets and companies not available on the ASX. The dividends would flow into the offset account against the non-deductible home loan, reducing interest on the portion that gave them no tax benefit. Over time, as dividends accumulated in the offset and the non-deductible balance fell, the structure would progressively shift their debt profile from passive to active.

Tess took three weeks to agree. She asked every question twice. She wanted to understand exactly what would happen if shares fell 30 per cent. She wanted to know the worst-case scenario, not the projections. When she was satisfied that the structure could survive a downturn without forcing a sale - that the dividends would continue, the tax deduction would continue, and the offset buffer would hold - she signed.

Craig, who had been ready to move since that Saturday morning, said nothing. He knew that Tess's caution was not a brake. It was part of the structure.

The first twelve months tested them. Not because anything went wrong with the strategy, but because the psychological shift was harder than either of them expected.

Their total debt, which had been falling steadily for eight years, had just increased by $120,000. Craig understood the mechanics - the money had moved from inside the house to inside a share portfolio, and the interest on the new portion was deductible - but Tess saw a bigger number on the statement and felt it in her body.

The share portfolio did what share portfolios do. It fell seven per cent in its first quarter. It recovered. It dipped again. The total value fluctuated in ways that the property valuation never visibly did, even though the property was equally volatile underneath - they simply never received a daily price update on the house.

Tess stopped looking at the portfolio after the second month. Craig checked it weekly, then fortnightly, then let it be. The dividends arrived quarterly and flowed automatically into the offset account. Because Craig was the higher-income earner, the investment debt and the associated deductions sat against his income. A PAYG withholding variation - lodged with the ATO -

reduced the tax withheld from his salary each fortnight, putting more cash into his hands immediately rather than waiting for a refund at tax time. That extra cash went straight into the offset. The detailed tax mechanics - why Craig holds the deduction, how the franking credits prevent double taxation rather than reduce tax, and the full calculations - are set out in the appendix. But the effect was clear: the strategy was redirecting dollars from the ATO into the offset, where they reduced non-deductible interest every single day.

The structure was working. But it required something neither of them had expected: the willingness to hold a position that felt uncomfortable while knowing, intellectually, that it was sound.

By the end of year two, the picture had clarified in ways that surprised them both. The share portfolio was up fourteen per cent in capital growth. The dividends - directed to the offset from day one, not reinvested-had contributed an additional $6,800 in cash sitting against the non-deductible home loan. The PAYG variation and tax benefits had delivered thousands more into the offset across the two years.

The non-deductible portion of their home loan had actually fallen faster than it would have under their old strategy of simply making extra repayments. The combination of dividends flowing into the offset, plus the extra take-home pay from the PAYG variation, meant more dollars reducing non-deductible interest than they could have generated through wages alone.

Tess ran the comparison herself. Under the old approach - every spare dollar thrown at the mortgage - they would have reduced the home loan by approximately $38,000 over the two years. Under the debt recycling structure, the non-deductible balance had fallen by $44,000, and they held a share portfolio now worth $137,000 against the $120,000 investment loan that funded it. When she netted the portfolio against the loan and added the extra home loan reduction, the debt recycling structure had put them roughly $23,000 ahead of where the old approach would have left them-in just two years. Not a life-changing number yet. But the gap would widen every year as the portfolio grew, the dividends compounded in the offset, and the non-deductible debt continued to shrink faster than it otherwise would have.

'We didn't just borrow more money,' Tess said, looking at the numbers. 'We made the money we already owed work differently.'

Craig said something simpler: "'We bought ourselves options.'

He was right. They now held a liquid share portfolio they could access within forty-eight hours if needed. They held an investment property generating rental income. Their non-deductible debt was falling faster than before. They had gone from a household with one strategy-pay down the mortgage-to a household with multiple engines running simultaneously.

Optionality... Not one path. Several.

Craig and Tess did not speculate. They did not borrow money they could not service. What they did was far quieter and far more powerful: they took on additional debt deliberately, directed it into income-producing assets, and let the Australian tax system reward them for the decision.

The difference between their old strategy and their new one was not the amount of risk. It was the amount of optionality. The mortgage-only couple has one outcome: a paid-off house and whatever super has accumulated by default. The debt-recycling couple has multiple outcomes, multiple income streams, and multiple points of flexibility that compound over time.

Optionality is not about taking more risk. It is about creating more paths to the same destination - and discovering, along the way, that some of those paths lead somewhere better than you originally planned.

THE AUSTRALIAN APPLICATION

Start Where You Are

Craig and Tess could debt-recycle because they had property equity to draw on. But what about the couple who does not own a home yet? The couple who is renting, saving, and wanting to start building wealth now - not after they have scraped together a deposit, navigated an auction, spent five years paying down a mortgage?

The answer is simple: *start where you are.* The two-engine system-property and shares... is the destination. But the order you build them in, and the speed at which you add each one, depends entirely on your circumstances. Some couples start with property and add shares later. Some start with shares and add property when the time is right. What matters is that they start.

This is where margin lending - used correctly, conservatively and with discipline - becomes a genuinely useful tool. Not the margin lending of leveraged speculators chasing momentum. The kind that the Dundee merchants would have recognised: structural, diversified, and governed by rules that prevent the market from forcing a sale.

A margin loan works differently from debt recycling. Instead of borrowing against property equity, you borrow against the value of the shares themselves. The lender provides a loan, secured by the portfolio, and the interest is tax-deductible because the borrowed funds produce assessable income. The risk is different too: if the portfolio falls below a certain loan-to-value ratio, the lender can issue a margin call-a demand for additional cash or a forced sale.

This is why the loan-to-value ratio matters more than anything else in margin lending. The couple who borrows at 70 per cent Loan-to-Value Ratio (LVR) is exposed to a margin call with even a moderate correction. The couple who borrows at 30 per cent LVR has a portfolio that would need to fall by more than half before a margin call is triggered. At that level, the structure can absorb the kind of volatility that the Australian share market has historically produced without ever forcing a sale.

The Couple Who Started With Shares

Nick and Jordan were renting a two-bedroom apartment in Marrickville when they came to see me in mid-2023. Nick was a graphic designer earning $95,000. Jordan worked in logistics for a freight company earning $105,000—combined income: $200,000. No property. No share portfolio. Two super accounts sitting in default options. A savings account with $64,000 that they had been building toward a deposit - though neither of them was sure a deposit was the right next step.

Sydney property prices felt unreachable. They had been saving for three years, and the deposit target kept moving. Every time they got close, the market added another $50,000 to the entry point. Jordan was frustrated. Nick was starting to wonder if the whole strategy was wrong.

"What if we stop chasing the deposit and start investing instead?" Nick asked during our first meeting. "We keep hearing that shares are the second engine. Why can't they be the first?"

They could. The point was not to abandon the idea of property. The point was to stop waiting. They could build one engine now and add the second when their circumstances allowed. The couple who waits five years for the perfect deposit while their savings sit in a bank account earning less than inflation has not been patient. They have been idle. Nick and Jordan did not want to be idle any more.

After talking this through, we structured a margin lending arrangement at 30 per cent LVR. Nick and Jordan invested $60,000 of their savings into a diversified portfolio of Australian and international ETFs. The margin lender provided an additional $26,000 in borrowings, bringing the total portfolio to

$86,000. The interest on the $26,000 was tax-deductible. The dividends flowed into their savings account. They retained $4,000 in cash as a buffer.

At 30 per cent LVR, their portfolio could fall by more than 55 per cent before a margin call was triggered. Across global share markets, a fall of that magnitude has occurred only once in modern history - during the Global Financial Crisis of 2008–09, when major indices fell approximately 50 to 55 per cent peak to trough - and every major market recovered within seven years. The structure gave them room to hold through anything the market was likely to produce.

Alongside the margin portfolio, they set up a $600 fortnightly automatic investment-$300 from each of them - buying additional ETF units at whatever the market offered. The regular contributions diluted the margin ratio over time, gradually reducing the LVR as fresh capital entered the portfolio. Within eighteen months, the LVR had fallen to 22 per cent without them paying down a dollar of the margin loan. The portfolio was derisking itself through the discipline of regular contributions.

The tax benefit was immediate. Jordan, as the higher earner at $105,000, held the margin loan in his name. The deductible interest reduced his taxable income. The franking credits attached to the Australian dividends ensured that income was not taxed twice - the company had already paid 30 per cent, which matched Jordan's marginal rate exactly, so no additional tax was owed on the franked portion. The international dividends were unfranked but still assessable income produced by deductible borrowings. The detailed mechanics are set out in the appendix.

Nick summed it up like this: "We spent three years saving for a house we couldn't afford. In eighteen months of investing, we've built more wealth than the savings account ever did. And when we're ready to buy, we'll have a bigger deposit because the portfolio grew."

Nick and Jordan did not skip property. They started building before property was ready for them. The first engine was running. The second would come when the time was right.

Superannuation: Important, But Not Necessarily Now

A note on superannuation, because it belongs in this conversation even if it is not the centrepiece of it.

Every Australian employee has a super account. A super account is a long-term investment account, funded primarily through compulsory employer contributions, that holds and grows money on your behalf until you reach preservation age. Most couples have two. Those accounts are invested - in shares, property, bonds, or a mix - inside the most tax-effective structure available in this country. Earnings inside super are taxed at 15 per cent. Concessional contributions are taxed at 15 per cent going in, compared to your marginal rate of 30 or 37 per cent outside super. The maths is compelling.

But for a couple in their thirties or early forties, maximising super contributions is not always the priority. Super is locked until preservation age. Every dollar that goes in cannot be accessed for decades. For a couple who is trying to build a deposit, fund a debt recycling strategy, maintain an offset buffer, or simply keep cash flow intact while running investment engines that they can actually touch - directing large voluntary contributions into super can create a liquidity problem that undermines the rest of the structure.

This depends heavily on the individual situation. A couple with strong cash flow and no immediate need for the capital may benefit from salary-sacrificing additional contributions now. A couple stretching to service a mortgage and an investment portfolio may be better served directing those dollars into the offset or the share portfolio where they remain accessible.

The principle is simple: super becomes more important as you move through your forties and into your fifties, when preservation age is closer, when your marginal tax rate is often at its highest, and when the concessional contribution caps offer the greatest tax arbitrage. For most couples in the early building years, the priority is the engines you can access-property, shares, offset - and super takes care of itself through compulsory employer contributions until the time is right to optimise it deliberately.

The couple who ignores super entirely is making a mistake. The couple who pours money into super at thirty-five while their offset is underfunded and their share portfolio is non-existent is also making a mistake. The answer, as with most things in this book, is structure - and the right structure changes as the household changes.

Your superannuation is not a retirement plan. It is your most tax-effective investment account - but knowing when to lean into it matters as much as knowing that it exists.

The Line Between Leverage and Recklessness

Not all debt-funded share investing is created equal, and the distinction matters enormously.

Debt recycling uses equity in a property you already own. The underlying security is bricks and land, not the shares themselves. If the portfolio falls 30 per cent, the lender does not force you to sell. Margin lending uses the shares as the security - which means a forced sale is possible if the portfolio falls far enough. But the risk of a margin call is a function of the loan-to-value ratio, not of margin lending itself. At 30 per cent LVR, the structure is conservative. At 70 per cent, it is fragile. The tool is the same. The discipline around it is what determines the outcome.

For the couple who owns property and has equity to deploy, debt recycling is the natural tool. For the couple who does not yet own property, or who is building one engine at a time, a conservative margin loan can serve the same structural purpose - turning idle capital into a working portfolio with deductible interest and franked income.

The Dundee merchants understood this. The trusts that survived were the ones that never allowed the market to force a sale. The trusts that failed were the ones where the structure demanded action at exactly the moment when inaction was the only sane response.

Leverage is a tool. Like any tool, it serves the disciplined and punishes the reckless. The question is never whether to use it. The question is whether the structure around it can survive the worst day without forcing a decision you'll regret for a decade.

WEALTH BUILDER REFLECTION

One question to sit with:

How much of our equity is actually working for us right now - and how much is sitting inside our home, growing passively, while we pay non-deductible interest on every dollar of it?

One truth to keep:

The couple with one strategy has one outcome. The couple with optionality has the freedom to choose - and in a decade of investing, that freedom is worth more than almost any single decision they will ever make.

Chapter 10 takes everything this book has built - property, shares, debt strategy, tax structure, superannuation - and asks the question that ties it all together:

what is the right mix for your household? The answer is not a formula. It is a conversation - and it starts with understanding where you are, not where someone else thinks you should be.

PART FOUR

Blending Property & Shares

CHAPTER 10

Finding Your Perfect Mix

Sequence matters more than speed

It is a Friday night in Hornsby, and Deepa and Arun are driving home from a dinner party in silence. They've just spent three hours listening to friends talk about money like experts (spoiler alert: they, unlike their friends, are not 'experts'). Now they are sitting quietly, each privately unsure whether they are doing anything right.

The dinner had started normally enough. But somewhere between the main course and dessert, the conversation had turned - as it always does among couples in their late thirties - to property, shares and indirectly... the question of who is getting ahead and who is falling behind.

Cameron and Jess, who had bought three investment properties in four years, had been the most confident voices at the table. They described their strategy as if it were self-evident: leverage, negative gearing, repeat. They hadn't looked at a single share. Why would they? Property is real. You can drive past it.

Toby and Kath had gone the other way. They owned their home and nothing else - but they had a share portfolio worth over $320,000 and growing, built entirely through automatic ETF contributions since their late twenties. No debt. No tenants. No stress. They described it with the satisfaction of people who had chosen the simpler path and felt vindicated.

Now, on Deepa and Arun's drive home, Arun is the one who speaks first.

'We have a property, and we have shares,' he says. 'But I honestly don't know if we have them in the right amounts. Or the right order. Or if we should be doing more of one and less of the other.'

Deepa nods. She has been thinking the same thing since the main course.

'Everyone at that table had a completely different strategy,' she says. 'And every single one of them sounded like they were right.'

They pull into the driveway. Neither of them moves to open the car door.

'What's our mix?' Arun asks. 'What's the right split between property and shares for us? Is there a formula?'

There is no formula. But there is something better than a formula. There is a sequence - and understanding it is the difference between building a portfolio that works as a system and assembling a collection of assets that merely coexist.

The right mix is not a number you calculate. It is a sequence you build - and the couple who gets the order right will always finish ahead of the couple who tries to do everything at once.

The Myth

This chapter sits at the hinge point of the book. Everything before it has introduced the individual pieces - property, shares, tax, debt, emotional resilience. Everything after it will turn those pieces into a plan.

But before the plan comes the question that keeps more Australian couples awake at night than any single investment decision: how much of each? How much property versus how much shares? How much debt versus how much equity? How much now versus how much later?

The financial industry treats this as a calculation. Risk profile questionnaires. Asset allocation models. Portfolio construction software that produces a neat pie chart and a reassuring percentage split. Sixty-forty. Seventy-thirty. Whatever the algorithm says.

Those tools are not useless. But they answer the wrong question. They answer *what* to hold. They do not answer *when* to build it.

And for the couple who is building from two incomes across a decade, the when matters more than the what. A portfolio that arrives in the right sequence - each new piece funded and protected by the ones before it - will outperform a portfolio that was theoretically optimal but built in the wrong order.

Sequence matters more than speed. This is the principle that governs this chapter, and it is the principle most couples discover too late - usually after they have tried to do everything at once and found that doing everything at once is the fastest way to do nothing well.

WEALTH BUILDERS THROUGH TIME

The Merchant Layers of Osaka - Japan, 1600–1800

In the early seventeenth century, as the Tokugawa shogunate imposed an enforced peace across Japan, a new class of merchant families began to emerge in the commercial heart of Osaka. They were not samurai. They held no political power. In the rigid social hierarchy of Edo-period Japan, merchants were formally ranked at the bottom - below warriors, farmers, and artisans.

But Osaka, known as the 'kitchen of Japan,' was where the nation's commerce actually happened. Rice from every domain in the country was shipped to its warehouses. Trade goods moved through its canals. And in the narrow merchant quarters along the Dōtonbori and Semba districts, families were quietly building fortunes that would outlast the samurai who looked down on them.

Among them was the Konoike family. Konoike Shinroku, the founder, began in the 1610s not in Osaka itself but in the nearby town of Itami, where he operated a sake brewery. It was a respectable business in a respectable town. Most brewers stayed brewers. The money was steady, the margins were known, and the ambition required to do anything more was considered, in a society that valued stability above all else, slightly dangerous.

Shinroku was not reckless. But he had a quality that separated him from the other brewers of Itami - a quality that would define his family for two hundred years.

He understood the difference between adding assets and sequencing them.

The Konoike family operated under a belief that was never formally recorded but was visible in every generation of their decisions: each new venture must be funded by the income of the last, and each new layer of wealth must be protected by the stability of the layer beneath it.

This sounds obvious. It is anything but. The natural instinct of every successful merchant - in Osaka in the 1600s, in Sydney in the 2020s - is to expand as quickly as capital allows. The sake is profitable, so borrow against the brewery and open a second one. The second brewery is profitable, so buy a third. Speed feels like progress. More feels like safety. But the Konoike understood that more, built on the wrong foundation, is not safe. It's dressed up as ambition, but really it's quite fragile.

Their belief was that the order mattered more than the speed. Do the right thing next - not everything at once.

The sequence the Konoike built across three generations was precise: The first generation brewed sake; it was a cash-flow business with manageable risk and steady demand. Rather than expanding the brewing operation aggressively, Shinroku used the income to fund a second, entirely different activity: shipping. He began transporting sake and other goods by sea from Itami to the growing port of Edo. The shipping income did not replace the brewery income; rather, it added another layer.

The second layer funded the third: As the Konoike became established shippers, they gained intimate knowledge of the rice trade - which commodities moved where, at what price, in what season. They became rice brokers, operating in the Osaka rice exchange that was, by the mid-1600s, one of the most sophisticated commodity markets in the world. Their brokerage commissions created a third income stream, uncorrelated with either brewing or shipping.

The third layer funded the fourth: The rice brokerage brought them into contact with the daimyō - the feudal lords whose rice revenues were converted into cash through the Osaka exchange. The Konoike began lending money to these lords, at first cautiously, then systematically. They became bankers. Not instead of being brewers and brokers and shippers - in addition to them. Each income stream supported the others. Each asset class operated in a different cycle. When shipping was slow, rice brokerage was busy. When brokerage margins compressed, the loans to the daimyō generated interest.

The fourth layer funded the fifth: With four income streams now running, the Konoike began acquiring land. Not speculative land. Income-producing land - agricultural holdings that generated rent and rice yields regardless of what happened in the commercial markets of Osaka. The land was the foundation beneath everything else. It could not be lost in a trade, called in by a creditor, or destroyed by a typhoon in the harbour.

At every stage, the Konoike faced pressure to move faster. Rival merchant houses in Osaka pursued concentration - the rice brokers who became nothing but rice brokers, the shippers who borrowed against their fleet to build a bigger fleet, the lenders who deployed every yen of capital into a single high-yield loan to a powerful lord.

Concentration produced spectacular short-term results. Some of those rivals grew faster than the Konoike in any given decade. But the Osaka merchant quarter was littered with the names of families who had risen quickly and fallen just as quickly - wiped out by a single bad harvest, a single defaulting lord, a single typhoon that destroyed a fleet they had not diversified away from.

The Konoike watched these families fail and understood something that speed-obsessed merchants never learned: the risk was not in any individual asset. The risk was in the sequence. A family that rushed from brewing directly to money-lending, without the intermediate layers of shipping and brokerage, had no fallback when the loans went bad. A family that moved from rice brokerage directly to land acquisition, without first building the income streams to service and protect that land, was one drought away from forced sale.

Each layer of wealth was only safe if the layers beneath it were established and functioning in the appropriate way as a foundational layer for the next.

The Konoike became one of the wealthiest merchant families in Tokugawa Japan. By the mid-eighteenth century, they held a portfolio that no single market disruption could threaten: brewing, shipping, brokerage, lending, and land. They survived famines that destroyed rice-only merchants. They survived shipping disruptions that ruined transport-only families. They survived the political upheavals that bankrupted families whose entire wealth was tied to loans to a single feudal lord.

Their wealth was not the largest in Osaka at any single point. That honour belonged, at various times, to more concentrated, more aggressive families who bet everything on the right trade at the right moment. But those families appeared and disappeared within a generation. The Konoike endured across two centuries.

When historians study the family, the consistent finding is the same: it was not what they owned that made them resilient. It was the order in which they acquired it.

The Konoike understood something that most wealth builders - in any era, in any market - learn too late. The decision of what to own matters less than the decision of when to add it. A land portfolio built before the income streams to protect it is a liability. A lending business launched before the operational knowledge to assess risk is a gamble. A shipping enterprise expanded before the capital reserves to absorb a loss is a single storm away from nothing.

Sequence creates resilience. Speed, without sequence, creates fragility.

The right move at the wrong time is still the wrong move.

The tools have changed. The principle hasn't.

An Australian couple in 2026 does not need to brew sake or broker rice. But the structural insight is identical. Property and shares, offset and debt recycling, tax strategy and time - each one is a layer. And the order in which those layers are built determines whether the system holds together under pressure or comes apart at the first serious test.

A PRESENT-DAY STORY

The Couple Who Tried to Build Everything at Once

Deepa and Arun - the couple from the dinner party - came to see me three weeks after that Friday night drive home from Hornsby. Deepa was a senior data analyst at a tech firm in Macquarie Park, earning $135,000. Arun was an Architect with his own firm in Epping, earning around $110,000. Combined household income was just over $245,000. They owned their home in Beecroft, purchased four years earlier for $1.15 million, now worth approximately $1.35 million. The mortgage sat at $760,000 with $42,000 in the offset.

They also held one investment property - a two-bedroom apartment in Wollongong they had bought eighteen months earlier for $530,000 - and a share portfolio of approximately $28,000 in a mix of individual Australian shares that Arun had selected himself based on articles he had read online.

On paper, they were doing well. Two assets. Two incomes. A share portfolio in its nascent stage.

But they arrived in my office overwhelmed with a list of things to do but with no real reason as to what to do in sequence and why all should be done for their situation.

Deepa placed the list on the desk. It was handwritten with slightly different shades of ink, which told me she had been thinking about this for a while.

The list read: consolidate the share portfolio into ETFs, set up debt recycling against the home equity, look at a second investment property in Brisbane, restructure the Wollongong loan to interest-only, build the offset buffer, and investigate a family trust.

Six initiatives. All of them, individually, were reasonable. None of them was wrong. The list was, on its face, the list of a couple who had done their research and understood the landscape.

But the list was also the problem.

Deepa and Arun believed - because every finance podcast and property seminar and investing blog had told them - that the key to building wealth was to do as much as possible, as fast as possible. That time in the market was everything. That every month they delayed a strategy was a month of compounding they would never get back. That the disciplined couple was the couple who ticked every box simultaneously.

This belief was not wrong in principle, but was catastrophically wrong in practice. Because doing six things simultaneously, for a couple with $42,000 in the offset and a share portfolio built on magazine tips, is not discipline. It is a recipe for a structure that cannot survive its first test.

I asked them to put the list away. Then I asked a different question.

'If you could only do one of those things in the next twelve months, which one would make everything else easier?'

They looked at each other. Neither of them had thought about it that way.

We spent the next hour working through the sequence. Not the list - the sequence. The order in which each move should happen so that every subsequent move was funded, supported, and protected by the one before it.

Step one was not exciting. Step one was building the offset to nine months of core household expenses - roughly $75,000. That meant their mortgage repayments plus insurance, utilities, groceries, and transport, multiplied by nine. They had $42,000 already. The gap was $33,000, and with every spare dollar directed into the offset, it would take approximately ten months to close.

Deepa resisted. 'We're losing ten months of compounding,' she said.

'You're buying ten months of structural stability,' I said. 'Everything you want to do after this becomes possible because of it. Without it, one rate rise, one vacancy period on the Wollongong property, one unexpected expense - and you're making decisions from panic instead of strategy.'

Step two, once the buffer was in place: sell the individual shares. Not to cash out - to redirect. The $28,000 from the sale would go straight onto the home loan, reducing the non-deductible debt. Then they would reborrow that same $28,000 as a separate investment loan split and invest it into two broad-based ETFs - one Australian, one international. Same money. Different tax treatment. The debt that had been costing them was now working for them, because interest on money borrowed to produce investment income is deductible. The non-deductible home loan shrank. The deductible investment loan replaced it. The share portfolio was rebuilt on a foundation that the tax system actually rewarded.

Step three, beginning immediately after the reborrow: every spare dollar now goes to paying down the home loan. Not the investment loan - the home loan. Every fortnight, every bonus, every tax refund. The home loan is the non-deductible debt, and every dollar paid off it is a dollar of dead weight removed from the structure. Simultaneously, restructure the Wollongong loan to interest-only. The cash flow saving - approximately $200 per fortnight - also goes onto the home loan.

Then, at the end of each year, they would redraw on the increased equity in the home - built from both the accelerated repayments and the property's capital growth - and invest the redrawn amount into the ETF portfolio. Another layer of non-deductible debt converted to deductible. Another layer of shares funded not by sacrifice but by the structure doing its work. Any dividends or distributions from the share portfolio would flow straight back onto the home loan, accelerating the cycle further.

They would also redraw on the growing equity in the Wollongong investment property, directing that capital into the share portfolio as well. Two redraws. Two sources of investment capital. Both feeding the same share engine while the home loan steadily shrank.

Arun asked the question I was expecting: 'When do we look at a second investment property?'

Not before eighteen months of the above strategy was running. And when they did, the property would go in Deepa's name. The reason was structural: by that point, Arun would hold the debt-recycled investments and the new borrowings in his name. Deepa's taxable income is now the highest in the household - Arun's reduced by the deductions flowing through the debt-recycled portfolio. If Deepa's income grows above $135,000 in the coming years, the deductions on the new property would work against her marginal rate of 37 cents in the dollar. Even at her current level, concentrating deductions on the partner with the most 'deduction capacity' within the bracket preserves flexibility for future moves.

The family trust stayed on the list, but at the bottom. Not because it was wrong - trusts can serve a genuine purpose for asset protection and for distributing income to other family members in lower tax brackets. But a trust adds complexity, compliance costs, and administrative overhead. For Deepa and Arun, at this stage, the structure would cost more to maintain than it would save. It was something to revisit in year three or four, once the debt recycling was mature, the second property was settled, and the portfolio was generating enough income to make the distribution benefits real.

Deepa struggled with the first six months. She was a data analyst by profession. She understood compounding mathematically. She could see, on a spreadsheet, what ten months of paused share contributions would cost over twenty years. The number was real, and it bothered her.

Arun's tension was different. He watched friends - including Cameron and Jess from the dinner party - buy their fourth investment property while he was still building a buffer. The comparison was quiet but persistent. He never said it out loud, but Deepa could see it in the way he read property listings on his phone on Sunday mornings.

The hardest part of the sequence was not doing the work. It was tolerating the feeling that they were falling behind while they were actually building the foundation that would let them move faster later. Then, nine months into the plan, the test arrived.

The Wollongong apartment sat vacant for four weeks between tenants. No rent. Full mortgage repayments. Body corporate levies still due. In the same period, Arun's fee revenue dropped fifteen per cent when a major residential project he was designing was put on hold after the developer's financing fell through, and two smaller commissions were delayed by council approval backlogs.

Four weeks of no rental income and reduced fee revenue, arriving simultaneously. Under their old structure - the $42,000 offset, the scattered share portfolio, the wish list of six simultaneous initiatives - this would have forced a decision. Pause something. Sell something. Retreat to safety.

Under the new structure, the offset absorbed the gap without requiring any change to the plan. They did not sell. They did not pause. They did not panic. The buffer did the work it was built to do.

'That's what ten months of boring discipline bought us,' Deepa said afterwards. She did not mention the spreadsheet again.

By the end of year two, the picture had clarified in ways neither of them had expected.

The home loan had dropped by $61,000 - far more than the scheduled repayments alone would have achieved. Every spare dollar, every dividend, every tax refund, and every cash flow saving from the Wollongong interest-only switch had been hammering the non-deductible debt. The offset, drawn down briefly during the vacancy period, had rebuilt to $68,000.

The share portfolio told its own story. The initial $28,000, recycled through the home loan and reborrowed, had been joined by two annual equity redraws and a redraw against the Wollongong property's growth. The portfolio now sat at $79,000, entirely in low-fee ETFs, with every dollar of borrowing cost tax-deductible. The franked dividends were flowing back onto the home loan, quietly converting non-deductible debt into deductible debt with every distribution.

The system was feeding itself. The more they paid down the home loan, the more equity became available to redraw and invest. The more they invested, the more dividends flowed back onto the home loan. Each layer was accelerating the one beneath it.

They had not yet bought a second investment property. But the conversation had shifted. Deepa was researching locations, and the loan would go in her name - her taxable income was now the highest in the household, with Arun's reduced by the investment deductions flowing through the debt-recycled portfolio. The negative gearing on the new property would work hardest against her marginal rate.

Cameron and Jess, the dinner party couple with four properties, called Arun one Sunday to ask if he knew a good financial adviser. They were over-leveraged. Two of their properties were running at significant negative cash flow. They had no share portfolio, no meaningful offset buffer, and no liquidity. A single rate rise had tipped them from confidence to quiet desperation.

They had built quickly, but they had not built in sequence.

Deepa and Arun did not find their perfect mix through a formula. They found it through a sequence. Each layer of their wealth system was built on the foundation of the one before it, and each layer made the next one safer, simpler, and more effective.

The buffer made the debt recycling possible. The debt recycling made the share portfolio possible. The share portfolio's dividends accelerated the home loan paydown. The home loan paydown created more equity to recycle. And eventually, when the structure was deep enough, the second investment property became possible - not because they rushed to buy it, but because by the time they did, every other layer of support was already in place.

The couple who builds in sequence does not finish last. They finish strongest. Because the couple who builds quickly but out of order will, at some point, face a test that reveals the gap in their foundation. And that test, in property and shares, always arrives at the worst possible moment.

THE AUSTRALIAN APPLICATION
The Advantage Hidden in Two Incomes

Every structural advantage this book has described - negative gearing, the CGT discount, franking credits, offset accounts - becomes more powerful when a couple uses their two incomes as a sequencing tool rather than treating them as a single pool.

This is the integration advantage that most Australian couples never see. Not because it is complicated, but because no one frames it this way.

Consider what two incomes actually allow. While one partner's earnings cover the household's commitments, the other's can be directed entirely toward building the next layer - attacking the home loan, funding redraws, absorbing a vacancy or a rate rise without breaking stride. The couple can maintain momentum on two fronts simultaneously. They are not choosing between defence and offence; they can do both.

It is a lot more difficult to do this as a single-income household, not impossible but not as easy. Every dollar serves one purpose at a time. Pay down the mortgage or fund the buffer. Service the investment property or contribute to shares. One disruption - a job loss, a rate rise, a vacancy - cascades across the entire system with no second engine to absorb the impact.

The dual-income couple does not face the same constraints that a single-income household does. They can absorb a disruption on one side without halting progress on the other. This is not a marginal advantage. Over a decade of investing - through rate cycles, vacancy periods, market corrections, and the ordinary disruptions of life - it is the structural edge that separates the couple who finishes the plan from the couple who abandons it halfway through.

How Two Incomes Change the Sequence

The sequencing strategy described in this chapter is not just for couples who feel overwhelmed. It is a structural framework that leverages the dual-income advantage at every stage.

1. In the first phase - building the buffer - two incomes mean the offset can be funded in months rather than years. A couple earning a combined $220,000 can build a nine-month buffer in ten to twelve months without dramatic lifestyle changes. A single-income household on $110,000 might need two years to reach the same position, delaying every subsequent step in the sequence.
2. In the second phase - debt recycling - two incomes give the couple a choice that a single-income household simply does not have: whose name carries the investment debt. The recycling can sit in one partner's name, concentrating the deductions against that partner's marginal tax rate while the other's income continues servicing existing commitments undisturbed. Or both partners can recycle in parallel, each drawing on their own equity and building their own portfolio. The right answer depends on income levels, tax brackets, and future borrowing plans - but the point is that the couple has the answer to choose from. The single-income household does not.
3. In the third phase - acquiring the next investment property - the dual-income structure allows the couple to place the asset in the name of the partner with the highest marginal tax rate, maximising the negative gearing benefit. Because one partner already holds the debt-recycled investments and the associated deductions, the other partner's taxable income is higher - and the new property's losses work hardest against that higher rate. Two incomes. Two names. Two strategic positions within one household.

At every stage, the second income is not just additional money. It is additional sequencing capacity - the ability to build the next layer while the current layer is still establishing itself, without either layer being starved of the cash flow it needs to survive.

The Investment Mix That Emerges

The right mix of shares and property for any couple is not a formula. It is the natural result of a well-built sequence.

A couple who follows the sequencing framework - buffer first, then debt recycling, then shares funded by equity redraws, then additional property - will arrive at a portfolio that is calibrated to their income, their risk capacity, and their life stage. Not because they chose the right percentage split, but because each decision was made at the right time, with the right foundation beneath it.

For most Australian dual-income couples in the income range this book is written for, the mix that emerges after a decade of sequenced building looks roughly like this: a family home with substantially reduced non-deductible debt and a well-funded offset, one or two investment properties generating rental income with strong equity positions, and a diversified share portfolio funded through debt recycling - producing franked dividends that continue to accelerate the home loan paydown.

The exact proportions will vary. They should vary. A couple with a higher-earning partner in the top tax bracket may weight more heavily toward negatively geared property. A couple with more moderate incomes may find shares and debt recycling deliver more value dollar for dollar. A couple closer to fifty may prioritise liquidity and income over growth.

The mix is personal and so is the sequence. No two couples will build in exactly the same order, because no two couples start in the same position. What matters is that each layer is built on the one before it - and that neither partner is white-knuckling the plan alone.

The perfect mix is not the one that makes you the most money. It is the one you can hold through a rate rise, a vacancy, and a bad quarter - without selling anything, without retreating, and without losing sleep.

Two incomes is not just more money. It is the ability to build two layers at once - and that ability, used with discipline across a decade, is the structural edge that turns an ordinary household into a wealth-building system.

WEALTH BUILDER REFLECTION

One question to sit with:
If we could only make one financial move in the next twelve months - not two, not three, just one - what would make the biggest difference to where we stand in fourteen years?

One truth to keep:
The right mix is not a number you calculate once. It is a sequence you build over time - and the couple who gets the order right will always finish ahead of the couple who tries to do everything at once.

Chapter 11 turns to the question that sits beneath every strategy in this book: debt. Not whether to use it - that question has been answered. But how to manage it across both assets, both incomes, and both sides of the ledger without letting it become the thing that breaks the system it was designed to build.

CHAPTER 11

Managing Debt Across Both

Stewardship beats status

It is a Thursday evening in Castle Hill, and Gemma is walking Bruce through the park as per usual.

She has been out for forty minutes but could not say where. The loan summary she printed that morning has followed her the whole way - not the paper itself, which is sitting on the living room table where she left it, but the number at the bottom. It has settled behind her eyes like a headache she cannot quite name.

She passes the woman with the two dachshunds and manages half a wave. The retired couple on the far bench call out to Bruce, and she barely hears them. She is drawn back along the footpath, up the driveway, through the front door, lead on the hook, water in the bowl, and there it is on the living room table—the printout.

A loan summary printed that morning from their broker's portal. Eighteen months ago, when she and Joel first sat down with an adviser, their total debt was $842,000. A home loan and a car loan. Two obligations. Simple.

Now the car loan is gone. Paid off in eleven months, exactly as they'd been advised. That part felt good. Genuinely good. The weight of a $38,000 liability at 7.9 per cent, attached to a depreciating Kia, lifted from their shoulders one Tuesday when the final payment cleared.

But in those same eighteen months, they'd also followed the rest of the advice. Purchased an investment property in Morphett Vale, south of Adelaide - deliberately interstate, deliberately in a market that moved differently to Sydney, because the whole point was not to have everything rising and falling at the same time. Set up a debt recycling facility against their home equity. Redirected $140,000 into a diversified ETF portfolio funded by redrawn equity.

Total debt on the summary in front of her: $1.37 million.

Gemma pushes the paper slightly away from her, like it might burn her. Joel comes down the hall from putting the kids down. He sees the printout on the bench. He sees her face.

'We followed the plan,' he says. It is not a question.

'We followed the plan,' Gemma says, 'and we owe half a million dollars more than we did before we started.'

She is not wrong about the number. She is wrong about what it means. But the feeling - the visceral discomfort of watching a debt figure grow when everything you were raised to believe says it should shrink - is not something you can talk someone out of with logic. It has to be shown.

'My parents worked their whole lives to get to zero,' Gemma says. 'They came here from Malaysia with nothing, bought a house in Eastwood, and paid it off in eleven years. They never invested. They never got advice. And they ended up okay. Not wealthy, but okay. Safe.'

She pauses.

'I don't want our kids to do it that way. I don't want them spending thirty years grinding to zero the way Mum and Dad did. That's why we're doing this. But looking at this number - it's hard not to feel like we've gone backwards.'

Joel sits down across from her and picks up the printout. After looking at it for a long moment, he says, 'Your parents spent thirty years getting to zero. We're trying to build five times what they had. That takes a different path. And a different path means carrying more debt along the way.'

He's right. But the path looking different is exactly the problem. And this chapter is about what happens when a couple has to hold their nerve through a number that feels wrong - because the structure underneath it is quietly, steadily, doing exactly what it should.

Not all debt is the same weight. The couple who knows which debt is working for them - and which is working against them - sleeps better and finishes richer than the couple who just sees a number.

The Myth

Gemma and Joel are not in trouble. They are, by any reasonable measure, ahead. Their combined income is $370,000. Their net asset position is strongly positive. The investment property is tenanted, the share portfolio is growing, the debt recycling structure is generating tax deductions and franked dividends. On paper, the system is working.

But paper is not where anxiety lives.

This is the tension that arrives for every Australian couple who builds across both property and shares. At some point - usually around year two or three of the plan - the total debt figure crosses a threshold that feels dangerous. Not because it is dangerous, but because the number is bigger than anything their parents ever carried, bigger than anything they imagined for themselves, and bigger than the number their friends who only own a home are carrying.

The temptation at this point is to retreat. Pay everything down. Sell something. Simplify. Return to the single-mortgage world that feels psychologically safe even if it is structurally slower.

This chapter is about why that temptation is understandable - and why acting on it is almost always the most expensive decision a couple in their position can make. Not because debt is inherently good. But because the couple who understands the hierarchy of their debt - which dollars are bad, which are good, and which are genuinely smart - will manage the weight without being crushed by it.

Stewardship is not the absence of debt. It is the disciplined management of what you owe, in service of what you are building.

WEALTH BUILDERS THROUGH TIME

The Quaker Merchants of England - Birmingham, York, and London, 1750–1870

In the middle decades of the eighteenth century, a network of Quaker families in the English Midlands were building businesses that would endure for over two hundred years. The Cadburys, the Frys, the Rowntrees, the Lloyds, the Barclays - names that survive today as global brands and institutions - began as modest traders in an era when religious dissenters were barred from universities, from Parliament, and from most of the social machinery that conferred status in Georgian England.

They could not buy their way into the establishment. They could not hold public office. They could not attend Oxford or Cambridge. The paths to respectability that defined the English gentry were closed to them by law and by custom.

What they could do was trade. And they did it with a philosophy that separated them from almost every commercial family of their era.

The Quaker faith held that wealth was not owned but held in trust. A family was a steward of its resources, not a proprietor. Ostentatious spending was not merely unwise - it was a spiritual failing. The meeting house enforced this: families who displayed excessive consumption were counselled, and those who did not reform were eventually disowned by the community.

This created a commercial culture unlike anything else in England at the time. While other merchant families used profit to buy estates, titles, and social position, the Quaker families reinvested almost everything back into the enterprise. Not because they lacked ambition. Because their ambition was pointed in a different direction. They were not building wealth to rise in society. They were building wealth to sustain their families, their workers, and their communities across generations.

And that distinction - stewardship over status - changed every decision they made about debt.

The Quaker merchants borrowed. This is important to understand, because the myth that has grown around them suggests a kind of monastic austerity that avoided debt entirely. They did not. The Cadburys borrowed to build their Bournville factory. The Lloyds borrowed to capitalise their bank. The Frys borrowed to expand their chocolate manufacturing.

But they borrowed with a discipline that their contemporaries found almost incomprehensible. Every pound of debt had to be productive - attached to an asset or an enterprise that would generate income sufficient to service the obligation and eventually repay it. Consumer debt was unthinkable. Debt taken for display, for comfort, for anything that did not produce a return was treated as a betrayal of the family's stewardship obligation.

They also maintained strict separation between the debts of different enterprises. A loss in one venture could not cascade into another. Each obligation was ring-fenced, each risk contained, each line of debt matched to the income stream that would service it. This was not sophisticated financial engineering. It was common sense, elevated to a principle by people who believed that the money was not theirs to gamble.

The tension was social rather than financial. In an era when every successful merchant family in England was converting commercial wealth into landed estates and aristocratic pretensions, the Quaker families refused. They lived in the same neighbourhoods as their workers. They drove modest carriages. They dressed plainly in an age of elaborate fashion.

Their peers thought them foolish. Why accumulate wealth if not to spend it? Why build a fortune if not to enjoy the status it conferred? The pressure to conform - to buy the country house, to educate the children at the right schools, to enter society - was relentless. Some Quaker families succumbed. The ones who did tended to lose their commercial discipline within a generation. The correlation was almost perfect: the family that began spending for status was the family that began borrowing for status, and the family that borrowed for status was the family that eventually lost the enterprise.

The families who held - who maintained the distinction between productive debt and consumptive debt, between building and displaying - are the ones whose names are still on buildings today.

By the mid-nineteenth century, the Quaker merchant network had produced an extraordinary concentration of enduring wealth. The Cadbury family had built one of the largest confectionery businesses in the world and an entire model village for their workers at Bournville. The Lloyd family had founded what would become one of Britain's largest banks. The Barclay family had done the same. The Rowntrees had built a chocolate empire and a philanthropic legacy that reshaped social policy.

None of them had bought a title. None of them had entered Parliament. None of them had built the grand country estate that every other successful English family of the era considered essential.

What they had done was something that looked quieter from the outside but was far more durable from the inside. They had managed debt as stewards - borrowing only for production, never for consumption, and holding each obligation against the income stream that justified it. When recessions came, when trade disrupted, when competitors failed, the Quaker families survived because their debt structure could absorb the shock. No single failure could bring down the enterprise, because no single debt was unsupported.

The Quaker merchants did not avoid debt. They disciplined it. They understood something that most families of their era - and most families in ours - never quite grasp: that the danger of debt is not its size but its purpose. A million pounds of productive debt, each pound attached to an income-generating asset, is structurally safer than ten thousand pounds of consumer debt attached to nothing but a lifestyle.

The families who borrowed for production survived for centuries. The families who borrowed for status survived for a generation.

The tools have changed. The principle hasn't.

An Australian couple in 2026 is not building a chocolate factory in the Midlands. But they face the identical structural question every time they look at their total debt: is this obligation productive or consumptive? Is it attached to something that generates income, growth, and tax advantage - or is it attached to something that loses value from the moment they sign the contract? The answer to that question determines whether the debt is building them up or quietly pulling them under.

A PRESENT-DAY STORY

What Changed When They Sat Down

When Gemma and Joel came to see me, the loan summary was the first thing she put on the table.

Joel was a mechanical engineer at a manufacturing firm in Smithfield, earning $120,000. Gemma owned and operated a community pharmacy in Ryde, clearing $250,000 after business expenses. Combined income: $370,000. They were thirty-eight and thirty-six, with one child in Year 2 and another starting school the following year. Their family home in Carlingford was worth approximately $1.65 million. Two super accounts totalled $310,000.

The assets were strong. The debt - $810,000 on the home, $416,000 on the Morphett Vale investment property, $140,000 in recycled debt funding the share portfolio - totalled $1.366 million. But the problem was not the debt. The problem was that Gemma was treating all of it as the same thing. And it wasn't.

What we did first was something I do with almost every couple who sits in that chair. We separated the debt.

Not on a spreadsheet. On a single sheet of paper, divided into three columns. Bad debt. Good debt. Smart debt.

Bad debt is the simplest category, and the one most people instinctively understand. It is debt attached to something that is depreciating, generating no income, and offering no tax deduction. Car loans. Personal loans. Credit cards. Buy-now-pay-later balances. Every dollar of interest on bad debt is pure cost. Gemma and Joel had already cleared their car loan on earlier advice - $38,000 at 7.9 per cent, gone in eleven months. That column was empty. The first piece of the structure was already in place.

Good debt sits in the middle. This is their home loan - $810,000 attached to an asset that is appreciating and provides the family's security and stability. The asset is real and growing. But the interest is not tax-deductible. Every dollar of interest on the home loan is paid from after-tax income. Good debt is not the enemy, but it is the most expensive debt to carry after bad debt is cleared. The strategy is twofold: build the offset account as a buffer, and then convert as much good debt as possible into smart debt through recycling. Every dollar that moves from the good column to the smart column stops costing you after-tax income and starts generating deductions instead.

Smart debt is the column that changed Gemma's face. The investment property loan: $416,000 at a higher interest rate, yes - but every dollar of interest was tax-deductible against Gemma's income. The Morphett Vale property was generating $21,840 per year in rental income. The depreciation schedule was producing a further $8,500 in non-cash deductions. The effective after-tax cost of holding this loan was roughly half what the headline interest rate suggested. The debt-recycled portion: $140,000 in equity redrawn from the home and invested in income-producing shares. The interest was tax-deductible. The shares were generating franked dividends. The franking credits were reducing Joel's tax. The structure was self-reinforcing.

Smart debt is not a weight. It is an engine. It is attached to assets that generate income, produce tax deductions, and grow in value. The interest you pay on smart debt is subsidised by the ATO. The assets it funds are compounding on your behalf. The couple who carries a million dollars of smart debt is in a fundamentally different position from the couple who carries a hundred thousand of bad debt - even though the first number is ten times larger.

When we tallied the three columns, the picture shifted.

Bad debt: zero.

Good debt: $810,000 - against a family home worth $1.65 million, partially neutralised by $187,000 in the offset.

Smart debt: $556,000 - against a $520,000 investment property and a $140,000 share portfolio. Generating income, deductions, and growth every single month.

The total was still $1.37 million. But the weight Gemma had been carrying was not the weight of recklessness. It was the weight of not knowing which column each dollar sat in.

'The number hasn't changed,' I said. 'But now you know what it's doing. Bad debt costs you. Good debt houses you. Smart debt builds you. They are not the same thing, and treating them as the same thing is the most expensive mistake you can make.'

The strategy we built from here was about one structural shift: converting good debt into smart debt - using the well-funded offset as the mechanism - without adding any bad debt back into the structure.

With $187,000 already sitting in the offset, the foundation was in place. I recommended the next move: take $60,000 from the offset, use it to make a lump sum repayment on the home loan - reducing the non-deductible balance from $810,000 to $750,000 - and then immediately redraw that $60,000 as a new investment-purpose split. The home loan balance returns to $810,000, but the purpose of that $60,000 has changed. It is no longer non-deductible housing debt. It is deductible investment debt. Good debt converted to smart debt, using the offset as the mechanism.

Joel was ready. Gemma was not.

'We just got the offset to a good place,' she said. 'Now you want us to take money out of it?'

'The offset will rebuild,' I said. 'But that $60,000 sitting in the offset is earning you the home loan rate - around six per cent, tax-free. Recycled into shares, it earns seven to ten per cent in growth and dividends, the interest on the redrawn portion becomes tax-deductible, and the franking credits reduce Joel's tax. The offset is doing one job. Recycled, the same dollars do three.'

Gemma took a week. She came back and said yes. Not because the logic had changed. Because she had sat with the three columns long enough to feel the difference between them, not just understand it.

The offset dropped to $127,000 after the withdrawal, and Gemma felt it immediately. She was used to seeing $187,000 on the screen. Now it read $127,000. The same discomfort she had felt about the total debt number - the visceral reaction to a figure moving in the wrong direction - arrived for the offset in reverse. Smaller felt dangerous, even though the structure underneath was now stronger.

But the system caught her. The $1,200 per fortnight that used to service the car loan - freed seven months earlier - was flowing into the offset. The PAYG variation from the investment property deductions was putting several hundred per fortnight back into their take-home pay, and that went into the offset too. The franked dividends from the now-larger share portfolio arrived each quarter and flowed straight in. Every dollar sitting in that offset was earning the equivalent of the home loan interest rate - tax-free. No savings account in Australia could match it.

Within months, the offset was climbing again. The share portfolio was generating $9,600 in annual franked dividends, and the PAYG variation had been updated to reflect the higher deductions - putting an additional $180 per fortnight into their take-home pay. The machine was feeding itself. The offset, which had bottomed at $127,000, had rebuilt to $135,000 and was still rising.

By the end of year two, the total debt had barely moved. It sat at $1.336 million. But the composition had shifted in a way that would have been invisible to anyone who only looked at the headline.

Bad debt: still zero.

Good debt: $720,000 - down from $810,000 (Sixty thousand converted to smart debt through the recycling, and a further thirty thousand paid down through regular principal repayments), neutralised by an offset of $140,000, effective interest running at under $2,900 per month, down from over $3,100 at the start.

Smart debt: $616,000 - up from $556,000, generating rental income, share dividends, franking credits, and tax deductions across both Joel's and Gemma's returns.

The $30,000 reduction in total debt came from regular principal repayments on the home loan, accelerated by the dividend income and PAYG variation savings flowing through the structure each fortnight.

The total debt was still large. But it was overwhelmingly smart. Every dollar of interest they were paying was either tax-deductible or offset by cash in the buffer. The structure was no longer a weight. It was an engine.

Gemma stopped walking Bruce past the park regulars without seeing them. Not because the number had disappeared. Because she understood what it was doing. And that understanding had replaced the anxiety with something quieter and far more durable: clarity.

'We don't owe less money,' she said. 'We just owe better money.'

Gemma and Joel did not eliminate their debt. They reorganised it. They moved from a structure where most of their borrowings were non-deductible - costing them after-tax dollars without generating income or tax advantage - to a structure where the vast majority of what they owed was attached to something that was growing, earning, and compounding on their behalf.

That is not recklessness. That is stewardship. The disciplined management of what you owe, directed entirely toward what you are building.

Different era. Same principle.

THE AUSTRALIAN APPLICATION

The Hierarchy That Changes Everything

The Australian tax system does something that most couples never think about clearly enough: it draws a hard, consequential line between debt that is tax-deductible and debt that is not. And on either side of that line, every dollar of interest you pay has a fundamentally different cost.

When you borrow to buy your family home, the interest is not tax-deductible. Every dollar of interest comes out of your after-tax income. If you are in the 45 per cent marginal bracket, you need to earn $1.82 to pay

$1.00 of home loan interest, because 45 cents of every dollar goes to the ATO before it reaches your mortgage.

When you borrow to buy an investment property or to invest in income-producing shares, the interest is tax-deductible. That same dollar of interest now costs you 55 cents in real terms, because the ATO effectively refunds the other 45 cents through your tax return - or through a PAYG withholding variation that puts the saving into your take-home pay each fortnight.

This distinction – deductible versus non-deductible – is not a minor technicality. Over a decade of investing, it is the single most important structural feature of Australian household debt. And most couples either do not know it exists or treat it as an accounting detail rather than what it actually is: the organising principle for every debt decision they will ever make.

The Three-Column Hierarchy

Every debt in a household falls into one of three columns, and knowing which column each dollar sits in determines how fast you build wealth and how well you sleep while doing it.

Bad debt sits in the first column. Car loans, personal loans, credit cards, buy-now-pay-later balances. These carry the highest interest rates, offer no tax deduction, and are attached to assets that depreciate or to purchases that have already been consumed. Every dollar of interest paid on bad debt is pure cost. There is no strategic argument for keeping it. The couple who still carries bad debt has no business expanding into investment debt. Clear it first. Clear it fast. Do not replace it.

Good debt sits in the second column. Your home loan, to the extent it is not offset by cash in the offset account, falls here. The interest rate is typically lower than bad debt, and the asset is appreciating, but the interest remains non-deductible. Every dollar paid here comes from after-tax income. The strategy is not to rush to pay this off entirely - that would mean diverting capital from productive uses - but to neutralise it with the offset and, where possible, to convert it into smart debt through recycling.

Smart debt sits in the third column. The investment property loan. The debt-recycled facility funding income-producing shares. These borrowings are attached to appreciating, income-generating assets, and the interest is tax-deductible. A couple in the 45 per cent bracket paying five per cent on a deductible investment loan is effectively paying 2.75 per cent after tax. In an environment where the underlying assets are returning seven to ten per cent, that debt is not a burden. It is an accelerant.

The hierarchy is not a suggestion. It is the structural logic of the Australian tax system applied to household debt. The couple who pays down smart debt before neutralising good debt is paying 45 cents in the dollar more interest than they need to, every single year, for every single dollar. That is not discipline. It is an expensive misunderstanding of how the system works.

Two Tax Rates, Two Sides of the Hierarchy

Chapter 10 described how two incomes let a couple build two layers of their wealth system in parallel. In debt management, that advantage becomes surgical - because two marginal tax rates let the couple assign each income to the side of the hierarchy where it works hardest.

Consider Gemma and Joel's structure. Gemma's income - the higher of the two, in the 45 per cent bracket - absorbed the investment property's carrying costs. Every dollar of deductible interest reduced her tax by 45 cents. The negative gearing benefit flowed back into their cash flow each fortnight through a PAYG withholding variation. The same deduction claimed against Joel's lower marginal rate would have returned less. The hierarchy demanded that the higher earner carry the smart debt, because the tax system rewards it more generously at the higher bracket.

It does not matter whose wages service which loan - the repayments come from the same household cash flow either way. What matters is whose name the deductible debt sits under. Gemma's income at the 45 per cent bracket turns every dollar of investment interest into a 45-cent deduction. The same interest claimed against Joel's 30 per cent bracket would return only 30 cents. Over a decade, that 15-cent difference on every dollar of smart debt compounds into tens of thousands of dollars in additional tax benefit - not because the couple earned more, but because they assigned the deduction to the right tax return.

This is the specific application of two tax rates to a debt hierarchy. The smart debt sits under the higher earner's name, where each dollar of interest generates the largest deduction. It is not about who makes the repayment. It is about who claims the deduction. The couple who structures their debt ownership this way - deliberately, not by accident - will pay tens of thousands of dollars less in tax over a decade than the couple who simply puts everything in one name or splits it down the middle.

The Three Rules of Debt Across Both

Managing debt across property and shares is not about complexity. It is about three principles applied consistently.

First: never carry bad debt alongside smart debt. Every dollar of interest on a car loan or credit card is unsubsidised, unproductive, and attached to nothing that grows. The couple who expands their investment portfolio while still carrying consumer debt is building on a cracked foundation. Clear the bad column before you grow the smart one.

Second: never confuse the size of the debt with the risk of the debt. A million dollars of smart debt against assets worth $1.8 million, generating $45,000 in annual income and $18,000 in tax deductions, is structurally safer than $50,000 of bad debt on a depreciating car. The number on the page is not the risk. The column it sits in is.

Third: always maintain the buffer before expanding the debt. The offset account is not optional in a leveraged structure. It is the load-bearing wall. A couple carrying $1.2 million of smart debt with six months of expenses in the offset can survive a vacancy, a rate rise, a job change, or a market correction without being forced into a bad decision. A couple carrying the same debt with no buffer is one disruption away from selling something they should be holding.

Debt is not the enemy. Unmanaged debt is. The couple who knows the hierarchy - who clears the bad, neutralises the good, and grows the smart - turns what feels like a weight into the quiet engine of everything they're building.

WEALTH BUILDER REFLECTION

One question to sit with:

If we sorted every dollar we owe into three columns - bad, good, and smart - what would each column hold? And what would it take, in the next twelve months, to move more of our debt from good to smart?

One truth to keep:

The couple who manages debt as a hierarchy - clearing what costs, neutralising what houses, and growing what builds - does not carry less weight. They carry it better. And over a decade, carrying it better is worth more than putting it down.

Chapter 12 takes everything this book has built - the principles, the structure, the stories, the hierarchy - and puts it into a single, actionable blueprint. Not a prediction. Not a projection. A process - designed for two incomes, two lives, and one shared commitment to building something that lasts.

PART FIVE

Your Action Plan

CHAPTER 12

Your 14-Year Blueprint

Process > predictions

Every chapter in this book opens the same way. Two people. A specific moment. A kitchen table, a car ride home, a laptop screen glowing in a dark room. You have read eleven of those openings, and by now you know what comes next: a story, a principle, a quiet shift in how you see the world.

This chapter is different. It's the chapter where the title earns its name.

Five times your wealth. That is the claim on the cover of this book, and if you have made it this far, you deserve to see exactly how it works. Not in theory. Not in projections drawn on a whiteboard in a seminar room. In practice - with real incomes, real growth rates, real tax mechanics, and a process you can follow from the first dollar to the last.

What follows are two paths. Two couples with the same starting position - $500,000 in investible funds - who build their wealth using the two engines this book describes: property and shares. One couple owns their home. The other does not. Their structures are different. Their plumbing is different. The Australian tax advantages they lean on are weighted differently.

Both at least reach 5X. Both do it with two engines - property and shares - running simultaneously.

Not because they predicted the right market. Not because they timed the cycle. Because they followed a process - the same process, year after year, through rate rises and corrections and headlines that told them to stop - and let the system do what systems do when you leave them alone long enough.

A note on the split: both couples divide their $500,000 roughly in half - about $250,000 into property, the rest into shares. This is not a rule. It is a simplification for the purpose of this chapter. A couple starting with $200,000 might weigh more heavily toward property first, because the proportion of the deposit for a property in Australia needs a higher deposit. A couple starting with $1 million might weigh more heavily toward shares, because with a large amount, you can have the deposit needed with a small portion of the starting amount. The principle is always the same: two engines, running together, compounding across time.

The couple who follows a process does not need to predict the future. They need to show up. And showing up, consistently, across fourteen years, is the strategy that has never stopped working.

PATH 1 - THE HOMEOWNERS

Hugh & Sana - Kellyville, Sydney

Who They Are

Hugh is forty-two. He runs project engineering for a mid-size construction firm in Norwest, earning $240,000. Sana is forty, an operations manager for a logistics company in Wetherill Park, earning $100,000. Combined household income: $340,000. Hugh sits in the 45 per cent marginal tax bracket. Sana sits in the 30 per cent bracket. They have been together for sixteen years, and they have two children in primary school.

They own their home in Kellyville, worth approximately $1.75 million, with $900,000 still owing on the mortgage and $100,000 sitting in the offset account. They have roughly $500,000 in usable equity - the gap between what the home is worth and the 80 per cent of its value a bank will lend against.

Their total investible position - the equity they can access by drawing the home loan to 80 per cent LVR - is $500,000. Separately, they keep $100,000 in the offset as their emergency fund. This money is not part of the $500,000.

It is not counted in the blueprint. It sits in the offset, reducing non-deductible interest on their home loan every day, and it buys them the ability to make no decision at all when the next disruption arrives.

The Deployment

The $500,000 is split roughly in half between the two engines.

1. First: $250,000 goes toward the deposit on an investment property - a new-build four-bedroom house in Springfield, Queensland. This is purchased for $1.25 million with a $1 million loan that represents 80 per cent LVR. A further $17,500 covers the unavoidable costs of acquisition: stamp duty on the land component of a new build, conveyancing, building and pest inspections, and loan establishment. This leaves $232,500 out of the initial $500,000 to deploy into shares.
   The property is brand new, which matters for one reason the couple did not initially appreciate: depreciation. A new build generates approximately $20,000 per year in non-cash depreciation deductions across the building structure and fixtures. This is a tax deduction for something the couple never actually pays. It only exists on paper, and it reduces their taxable income as if it were a real expense. Combined with the interest, rates, insurance, and management costs, the property generates a significant tax-deductible loss in the early years - all flowing against Hugh's income at 45 cents in the dollar.

2. Second: the remaining $232,500 is deployed into a diversified portfolio of Australian and international ETFs - 60 per cent international, 40 per cent domestic. This is not invested on day one. It is dollar-cost averaged across twelve months - roughly $19,400 per month - because no one, including the couple, knows what the market will do in the next quarter, and spreading the entry removes the need to care. The portfolio is built gradually across twelve

months, which means the increase in value of the portfolio and dividends (returns gotten from it) in the first year will be roughly half. Which just means the full $232,500 is only working for half the year.

This is why the appendix shows a deliberately modest year one: the engine is still being assembled. From year two onward, it runs at full power.

The entire $500,000 deployed - the deposit, the costs, and the shares - comes from a structured redraw against the home, drawing the mortgage from $900,000 up to $1.4 million at 80 per cent LVR. Because these borrowed funds are all invested in income-producing assets, the interest is tax-deductible from day one. This is debt recycling - the same mechanism described in Chapter 9. The recycled share-debt interest rate is assumed equal to the home loan rate - approximately 6 per cent in this model, in line with typical debt-recycling structures at the time of writing.

But this is only the beginning of the recycling, not the end of it. Each year the home grows, and each year that growth is drawn back down to its 80 per cent limit and pushed into the same portfolio - roughly $177,000 in the second year, another $165,000 in the third once a scheduled recycling top-up is added, tapering to around $78,000 across the fourth and fifth. By the end of year five, the deductible investment debt has grown from the original $500,000 to approximately $920,000, every dollar of it borrowed against appreciating assets, every dollar of it invested. And then it stops. Not by choice, but by design: the total investment debt reaches the ceiling a responsible lender allows - six times the household income - and the redraw lever quietly switches off. From that point the portfolio no longer grows by borrowing. It grows by compounding.

The emergency fund - $100,000 - stays in the offset. It is not touched. It is not invested. It is the structural element that makes everything else sustainable.

One structural detail that matters more than it appears: every investment debt - the recycled share loan, the investment property loan - is held in Hugh's name. Not because Sana is excluded from the strategy, but because Hugh sits in the 45 per cent marginal tax bracket. Every dollar of deductible interest, every dollar of depreciation, every dollar of negative gearing loss is worth 45 cents back through Hugh's return. In Sana's name, at 30 per cent, the same deductions would return 30 cents. The difference across fourteen years of compounding deductions is measured in tens of thousands of dollars. The assets belong to the couple. The debt belongs to the higher bracket.

The Annual Process

Once a year - spread across a week of appointments with their mortgage broker, accountant, and financial adviser, not crammed into a single evening - Hugh and Sana follow the same process:

They revalue the home. As the property appreciates, new equity becomes available at 80 per cent LVR. At 5 per cent annual growth, a $1.75 million home creates roughly $70,000 in new accessible equity each year - until the strategy's total investment debt reaches the limit a bank will responsibly lend, at which point this lever pauses, and the others keep pulling. They draw it down and invest it in the same diversified ETF portfolio. The interest on each new drawdown is tax-deductible from day one because the funds are used for income-producing investments.

Every two years, they debt-recycle. Here is how this works in practice: the dividends, franking credit refunds, and PAYG withholding variations that flow from the system throughout the year are directed into the home loan - paying down the non-deductible balance. Then, every two years, they redraw that accumulated amount and invest it in shares. The total debt stays the same. But the composition changes - less non-deductible, more deductible. Each cycle shifts the tax treatment further in their favour. In years where the tax deductions are particularly large, they have the option to pay down additional non-deductible principal, creating an even larger pool to recycle next time.

Alongside this, they contribute $20,000 per year from income - roughly $770 per fortnight between them. This is not a contribution to the share account. This is the cost of running the system. The interest payments, the IP shortfall, the carrying costs - they arrive monthly, before the tax system returns a cent. The $20,000 covers those costs as they fall due. In the early years, most of it services interest and carrying costs. As the system becomes cash-flow positive - typically by year four or five - more of the $20,000 flows directly into the share portfolio. Over the fourteen years, some years the contribution pays interest. Some years it buys shares. Every year it keeps the machine running. Every dividend, every franking credit refund, every PAYG withholding variation is channelled through the system. The system feeds itself.

One thing they do not do in this model: draw on the investment property's growing equity. As the Springfield property appreciates, new equity accumulates inside it, untouched. If they chose to redraw the IP to 80 per cent LVR each year and reinvest that equity, the returns would accelerate further. The model does not include this. The 5X does not require it. But the option exists - and for the couple who wants to push beyond 5X, it is the next lever to pull.

What It Actually Costs

Before the growth story begins, the couple needs to see what this system actually costs to run because it does cost, and they will feel it in the first few years.

In year one, the investment property costs approximately $70,000 to hold - $60,000 in interest on the $1 million loan, plus $10,000 in rates, insurance, and management. Against that, rental income brings in approximately $50,000. The gap - $20,000 - comes from the household. The share portfolio generates approximately $30,000 in deductible interest on the recycled share debt through the year. Because the portfolio is built gradually - dollar-cost averaged across twelve months rather than invested as a lump sum - the first year earns only a partial year of dividends, roughly $5,000. The net share-side cost in year one is around $30,000. Total out-of-pocket cost across the whole system in year one: approximately $50,000.

That is real money leaving the household every month. But then the tax system returns most of it. The investment property's deductible loss - the cash shortfall plus $20,000 in non-cash depreciation on the new build - combined with the deductible interest on the share debt and franking credits on the Australian dividends, generates approximately $32,000 in annual tax benefits. These flow back through Hugh's PAYG withholding variation fortnightly - not as a lump sum at tax time, but as reduced tax taken from every pay cycle across the year. The full component breakdown is in the appendix.

The real after-tax cost of running the entire system in year one: approximately $18,000 - the cash shortfall of roughly $50,000 reduced to a fraction of itself once the tax system returns its share. The $20,000 annual contribution covers it with a little to spare. And as rents grow and dividends increase over the years, even this gap closes. By year four, the system is cash-flow positive - generating more income than it costs to maintain.

Here is the distinction that changes how the couple experiences the process: cash flow is not wealth. In the early years, cash flow is tight. The bank account feels thinner. The monthly budget is working harder. But the couple's wealth - the net value of what they own minus what they owe - is growing at a rate their salary alone could never produce. The property is appreciating. The share portfolio is compounding. The equity is building silently, inside assets they own, while the cash-flow noise makes it feel like nothing is happening.

Cash flow is what you feel. Wealth is what you build. The couple who confuses the two will sell too early, stop too soon, or never start at all. The couple who understands the difference will keep showing up - because they know that the tighter months are the price of the compounding years.

This is why the $20,000 annual contribution exists. It is not an investment into shares. It is the servicing cost of the strategy - the cash that covers the interest payments, the IP shortfall, and the carrying costs as they fall due each month. The PAYG withholding variation returns a significant portion through the pay packet fortnightly. The annual tax return catches up the rest. Over the course of each year, the $20,000 is largely refunded by the tax system. But someone has to pay the bills while the system catches up - and that someone is the couple, from their income, month by month. The contribution is the bridge between when the costs arrive and when the tax benefits return. Without it, the system is not affordable. With it, the system is self-sustaining.

The First Five Years

At the end of year one, after the DCA is complete and the first equity top-up has been drawn, Hugh and Sana hold a share portfolio worth approximately $246,000 and an investment property worth $1.31 million. Their emergency fund sits untouched at $100,000 in the offset. Their total net investible position - assets minus investment debt - is approximately $59,000.

It does not feel like much. It does not feel like 5X. They have deployed half a million dollars, taken on significant debt, built a structure that requires a week of professional attention each year, and their net position has barely moved on paper. Sana's brother, who left their own funds of about $500,000 in his mortgage, seems to be in a better position initially.

This is where most couples lose their nerve. The first two years of the process feel indistinguishable from doing nothing. The share portfolio fluctuates.

The investment property costs money every month - though less than it appears, because the depreciation deductions are returning thousands each year in non-cash tax benefits. The total debt number - the one that sits on the bank statement - is larger than it has ever been. The system is working. It just does not look like it yet.

By the end of year three, the picture had shifted. The share portfolio, fed by equity top-ups, income contributions, recycled tax benefits, and reinvested dividends, has grown to approximately $661,000. The investment property is worth $1.45 million. The new-build depreciation has delivered over $60,000 in non-cash deductions across three years, all flowing through Hugh's return at 45 cents. The net investible position has reached approximately $267,000 - still only half the starting capital.

By the end of year five, the numbers tell a story that will test the couple's nerve. The share portfolio has reached approximately $880,000 - but the recycled investment debt that built it now stands at $920,000. On the share side alone, they are barely even. Five years of contributions, drawdowns, and reinvested dividends, and the portfolio has not yet outgrown its own debt. The real wealth so far is sitting quietly in the investment property - approaching $1.6 million, with $595,000 of equity - and in a share portfolio that is fully loaded and compounding, but not yet ahead. Annual dividends already exceed $30,000. The tax deductions from the combined debt structure - property interest, depreciation, recycled share-debt interest, franking credits - are returning close to $40,000 a year. Everything is in place. Nothing has yet paid off.

Net investible position at year five - shares and property, less all investment debt - approximately $560,000. A little over 1X. After five years of disciplined effort, they have roughly what they started with, plus a little. This is the number that breaks people.

A little over 1X in five years does not look like five times in fourteen. This is the moment the process asks the most of the couple - and it asks it precisely because the scoreboard looks so unconvincing. The temptation to change something - to sell the property, to stop the contributions, to chase a strategy that promises faster results - is strongest exactly here, at the bottom of the curve, where five years of effort have produced almost nothing visible. But the couple who changes strategy at the five-year mark is the couple who resets the compounding clock to zero. They quit one year before the engine they spent five years building finally turns over. And compounding does not forgive restarts.

Years Six to Fourteen

What happens next is the reason this book exists. In years six through ten, the system does something that feels, to the couple living through it, like a different strategy entirely. But it is not a different strategy. It is the same process - the same annual equity top-up, the same biennial debt recycling, the same $20,000 in contributions, the same reinvestment of every dividend and every tax refund. The only thing that has changed is the base on which the compounding operates.

A million-dollar share portfolio growing at 10 per cent generates $100,000 in new value in a single year. A $1.75 million investment property growing at 5 per cent creates close to $90,000 in new equity. The dividends - climbing from $35,000 toward $50,000, $60,000, $78,000 per year as the portfolio swells - are a river of capital flowing back through the loan structure and out again as freshly recycled, tax-deductible investment debt. In the early years, the couple also drew new equity from their home as it rose; by now that lever has reached the limit a responsible lender allows, and the home simply grows, its equity building untouched past $2 million and toward $3 million.

The couple is not working harder. They are not contributing more. The process is identical. But the system has reached the point where its own output exceeds the couple's input by a factor of three. The machine is running itself.

By the end of year fourteen, Hugh and Sana hold a share portfolio worth approximately $2.17 million, against recycled investment debt of $920,000—net share equity: $1.25 million. The investment property in Springfield is worth approximately $2.47 million against its $1 million loan - equity of $1.47 million. The emergency fund sits untouched at $100,000 in the offset, exactly where it started - additional to the investible position below.

Total net investible position: approximately $2.72 million (excluding the emergency fund, which remains untouched at $100,000).

5.4 times the starting capital. In fourteen years. On $20,000 a year in servicing contributions - and a process that took one week a year to maintain.

And they have not touched the investment property's equity. If they had drawn Springfield to 80 per cent LVR each year and reinvested, the number would be higher still.

The full year-by-year calculations - every equity top-up, every debt recycling event, every dividend, every depreciation deduction, every tax benefit - are set out in the appendix. The growth assumptions - 5 per cent property, 6 per cent share capital growth, 4 per cent dividend yield - are below the long-term Australian averages. The outcome is not the product of optimistic projections. It is the product of a process, followed consistently, across time.

PATH 2 - THE RENTERS

Luca & Dani - Ashfield, Sydney

Who They Are

Luca is forty-one. He is an IT director for a mid-size financial services firm in the CBD, earning $230,000. Dani is thirty-nine, a builder running a small residential construction crew in the inner west, earning $110,000. Combined income: $340,000. Luca sits in the 45 per cent marginal tax bracket. Dani sits in the 30 per cent bracket.

They do not own a home. They rent a two-bedroom apartment in Ashfield for $720 per week. This is not a failure of discipline. Luca migrated from Italy at twenty-eight. Dani grew up in Launceston and moved to Sydney at thirty. By the time they had combined savings and combined income, Sydney house prices had moved beyond what felt responsible for a couple still building their careers in a city they might not stay in forever.

They have $500,000 in savings and liquid investments. They are ready to stop waiting.

There is something worth pausing on here, because it runs against the assumption most people carry. A renter with half a million dollars in savings is not unusual - in fact, in my experience it is more common than a homeowner with the same amount sitting in cash. The reason is simple. The discipline that lets a couple rent modestly while their income climbs is the same discipline that builds a cash balance. Every dollar not committed to a mortgage, not swallowed by stamp duty, not locked behind the walls of a house, stays liquid. It accumulates. Homeowners, by contrast, tend to have their wealth in exactly one place: the home. Ask a homeowning couple for $500,000 in cash, and most cannot produce it without selling or borrowing - it is in the bricks. Ask a disciplined renting couple, and a surprising number can. Luca and Dani are not an exception. They are a type I have sat across from many times: people who chose flexibility over ownership, kept saving while they waited, and now hold something most homeowners do not - options, in cash, ready to deploy.

The Deployment

The $500,000 is split roughly in half between the two engines, just like Hugh and Sana's, but the plumbing is entirely different.

1. First: $250,000 goes toward the deposit on an investment property - a new-build three-bedroom house in Kingston, south of Hobart, purchased for $1.25 million with a $1 million loan at 80 per cent

LVR. As with Hugh and Sana, roughly $17,500 covers stamp duty, conveyancing, inspections, and loan setup, leaving $232,500 for the share portfolio. The loan is in Luca's name, with Dani as guarantor - a structure that uses their combined borrowing capacity even though the title sits with one partner. The property generates the same new-build depreciation benefits as Hugh and Sana's - approximately $20,000 per year in non-cash deductions, flowing against Luca's income at 45 cents in the dollar. The appendix sets out how this works.

2. Second: $250,000 goes into the same diversified ETF portfolio - 60 per cent international, 40 per cent domestic - dollar-cost averaged across twelve months. Alongside this, Luca and Dani establish a margin lending facility at a 22 per cent loan-to-value ratio. The margin lender provides approximately $66,000 in additional borrowed capital, bringing the total portfolio to roughly $298,000 once the DCA is complete. At 22 per cent LVR, the portfolio would need to fall by nearly 70 per cent before a margin call is triggered - a once-in-a-generation event. The margin interest - charged at approximately 9.5 per cent, in line with typical Australian retail margin lending rates at the time of writing - is fully tax-deductible because the borrowed funds produce assessable income. At a 45 per cent marginal rate, the after-tax cost of that 9.5 per cent is just 5.2 per cent. The shares return 10 per cent. The spread is positive from day one.

There is no offset account, because there is no home loan. So where does the emergency fund sit? Inside the investment loan facility itself. Luca and Dani maintain a cash reserve within the margin account. While this technically reduces the deductible loan balance temporarily, it is still a better home for emergency cash than a savings account; it offsets interest on a deductible loan, it is accessible within twenty-four hours, and it avoids the tax friction of earning assessable interest in a separate deposit. The appendix explains this structure in detail.

The Annual Process

Luca and Dani's annual process mirrors Hugh and Sana's in rhythm but differs in mechanics. They spend the same week across the year with their professionals - broker, accountant, adviser - reviewing the system and executing the next cycle.

Each year, as the share portfolio grows, the loan-to-value ratio on the margin facility falls. A $321,000 portfolio with $71,000 of margin starts at 22 per cent LVR. After a year of 10 per cent total returns plus contributions, the portfolio might be worth $385,000 - but the margin is still $71,000, so the LVR has dropped to 18 per cent. Luca and Dani top the margin back up to 22 per cent, borrowing an additional amount and investing it in the portfolio. The new margin is deductible. The portfolio grows. The LVR drops. They top up again.

This is the share-market equivalent of Hugh and Sana's annual equity top-up. The property creates new equity through growth; the portfolio creates new margin capacity through growth. Different asset, same principle: the system's own growth generates the capital for the next year's deployment.

They contribute a total of $20,000 per year from their joint income. Every dividend, every franking credit, every tax refund from the combined deductions of the margin interest, the investment property interest, and the new-build depreciation is reinvested. The system feeds itself.

The First Five Years

Year one feels slow for Luca and Dani like it did for Hugh and Sana, because the DCA means the full portfolio is not deployed until month twelve and the margin top-up does not kick in until the first anniversary. By the end of year one, the share portfolio sits at approximately $328,000 with a margin of $66,000 and the investment property is worth $1.31 million.

By year three, the margin top-up cycle has begun to compound. Each annual top-up is larger than the last because it is calculated on a larger portfolio. The share portfolio has reached approximately $506,000 with a margin of $135,000. The investment property is worth $1.45 million. Net investible position: approximately $818,000. The renter path is already ahead of the homeowner at this stage because the $232,500 in shares is equity from day one, not recycled debt. For that reason, it carries no interest drag. That advantage holds, and grows, for the whole journey.

By year five, the portfolio stands at approximately $707,000 with a margin of $191,000. Net share equity: $516,000. The investment property is approaching $1.6 million with equity of $595,000. The annual dividends from the portfolio are now funding most of the margin interest, and the franking credits are returning thousands each year through the tax system. Net investible position: approximately $1.11 million.

The same quiet moment arrives. A little over two times in five years. Their friends who bought a home are watching their mortgage fall. Their colleagues who chose term deposits are earning guaranteed returns with no anxiety. The process does not feel fast. It feels, if anything, like it is barely moving.

Luca and Dani keep going with the process.

Years Six to Fourteen

The margin top-up mechanism, which looked modest in the early years, becomes the primary growth engine in the second half of the journey. A million-dollar portfolio growing at 10 per cent generates $100,000 in new value. At 22 per cent LVR, that growth unlocks roughly $38,000 in new margin capacity each year. Added to the $20,000 servicing contribution and the $30,000-plus in dividends being reinvested, the system is deploying over

$90,000 of new capital annually by year seven - more than half of what Dani earns in a year.

The portfolio climbs through $1.1 million in year eight. Through $1.5 million in year ten. By year fourteen, the share portfolio stands at approximately $2.66 million, with a total margin of approximately $724,000. Net share equity: $1.94 million. The investment property in Kingston is worth approximately $2.47 million against its $1 million loan - equity of $1.47 million.

Total net investible position: approximately $3.41 million.

6.8 times the starting capital. Same process. Same contributions. Different plumbing - and, on the investible scoreboard, an even higher number than the homeowner reached.

The detailed year-by-year model for Luca and Dani - every margin top-up, every dividend reinvestment, every depreciation deduction, every tax benefit - is in the appendix alongside Hugh and Sana's. The growth assumptions are identical. The mechanism differs: home equity versus margin capacity. And the renter's investible number actually finishes higher - 6.8X against the homeowner's 5.4X - for one reason worth understanding. Luca and Dani's share capital is money they owned. Hugh and Sana's was borrowed from their home, carrying interest every year. Less drag, more compounding. But before any renter reads this as a verdict - that renting wins - there is one more number to put on the table. It is the number that changes the whole picture, and it is the subject of the next few pages.

WHAT HAPPENS WHEN THE NUMBERS DON'T COOPERATE

The numbers in both paths assume 5 per cent property growth and 10 per cent total share returns, applied evenly, every year, for fourteen years. Reality does not work like that. You already know this. The question is whether it matters.

It does not. And here is why:

In a real decade, there will be years where the property sits flat or dips. No new equity at 80 per cent LVR. No top-up. The couple who built their process around the annual equity drawdown simply skips that step and keeps contributing from income, keeps reinvesting dividends, keeps the system running on its other engines. The process does not break. One lever pauses. The others keep pulling.

There will be years where the share market drops fifteen per cent. The margin top-up is not available - the LVR has risen, not fallen, and adding leverage into a falling market would be reckless. The couple does the same thing: keeps contributing, keeps reinvesting dividends at lower prices, and waits. The units purchased during the downturn - bought automatically, without prediction, at whatever the market offered that fortnight - will be the best-performing units in the entire portfolio when the recovery comes. They always are.

And there will be years where the property jumps 12 per cent and the share market surges 18 per cent. In those years, the annual equity top-up is larger. The margin capacity is greater. The system deploys more capital, faster, without the couple changing anything they do. The good years do not require the couple to be clever. They require the couple to be present - to have the process in place so the system can capture the upside automatically.

Over many years, the flat years and the strong years average out. The long-term returns for Australian property and a blended global share portfolio - the returns on which this chapter's assumptions are built - are not projections of what might happen. They are observations of what has happened, across decades that contained recessions, rate shocks, pandemics, and financial crises. The appendix runs both paths through two full 14-year windows of actual returns - one share-poor era spanning the dot-com crash and the GFC, and the most recent fourteen years - to show how the system behaves when the market does what the market actually does.

The process does not require every year to be a good year. It requires the couple to keep showing up in the years that are not.

The bad years are not interruptions to the process. They are part of it. The couple who keeps contributing during a flat market is buying the same assets at lower prices. The couple who keeps holding during a correction is refusing to make a temporary decline permanent. And the couple who resists the urge to accelerate during a boom - who sticks to the process instead of chasing the cycle - is the couple who will still be building when the cycle turns.

TWO PATHS. ONE SYSTEM.

Hugh and Sana are homeowners who used the equity in their property as a capital deployment engine. Luca and Dani are renters who used the growth in their share portfolio as the same engine. One couple debt-recycled. The other used a conservative margin facility. One had an offset account sheltering their emergency fund. The other kept their buffer inside the investment loan facility. The structures are different. The result is not.

Both couples deployed $500,000. Both split it roughly in half between the two engines - property and shares. Both contributed $20,000 a year from income to service the system. Both reinvested every dividend, every franking credit, and every tax deduction the system generated. Both followed the same annual process - a week a year with their professionals, spread across the calendar. Neither predicted the market. Neither timed a cycle. Neither made a single decision that required foresight, brilliance, or luck.

They followed the process. The process delivered at least 5X.

This is a conservative outcome - the result of a system run with disciplined inputs and a 10 per cent share assumption that sits below the long-run average. Couples who push beyond it, by drawing the investment property's growing equity each year, contributing more from income, or running into stronger-than-average cycles, reach higher still. For readers who want to see the system tested against real data rather than smoothed assumptions, the appendix runs both paths through two full 14-year windows of actual Australian market returns - 1998–2011 and 2012–2025. Share returns use a 60/40 blend of the MSCI World ex-Australia Index in AUD and the S&P/ASX 200 Accumulation Index. Property returns use the ABS Residential Property Price Index and Cotality data. The 1998–2011 window is the more revealing: shares returned barely 5 per cent a year through two major crashes, yet both couples still cleared 5X - because the property engine and the reinvested tax benefits carried the years the share market could not. The 2012–2025 window, with a stronger share market, cleared it comfortably. Across the two windows, the system passed 5X through the dot-com collapse, the GFC's minus-40-per cent crash, multiple property corrections, a global pandemic, and the sharpest rate-tightening cycle in a generation. The crashes are not hypothetical. They are in the data, and the system absorbed them.

And here is what makes this system remarkable: most of the work is done not by the $20,000 the couple adds, but by the structure itself. The equity top-ups, the margin top-ups, the dividends, the franking credits, the depreciation deductions, the negative gearing refunds - all reinvested - do the heavy lifting. With no contributions at all, the system still compounds past five times the starting capital on its own. The $20,000 a year lifts the result further and shortens the road - but the engine, once built, largely runs itself. The contribution is the carrying cost of a wealth-building machine, and a modest one relative to what the machine produces.

But what if the couple wants more? What if they can direct more income into the system - not because they must, but because they choose to?

Annual Contribution	Homeowner Path	Renter Path
$0 (system only)	~5.23X	~5.6X
$5,000	**~5.24X**	**~5.8X**
$10,000	**~5.26X**	**~6.1X**
$20,000 (this chapter)	5.44X	6.8X
$30,000	~5.98X	~7.5X

The table makes the point that the chapters before this one have been building toward: the system is the strategy. Contributions accelerate it. Discipline amplifies it. But the structure - two engines, tax advantages reinvested, leverage maintained - is what builds the wealth. A couple contributing $30,000 per year does not just add $420,000 over fourteen years. They add it inside a system already generating its own fuel. The result is not 5X plus a bit more. For the homeowner, it is 6X; for the renter, closer to 7.5X - and climbing. The structure turns ordinary contributions into extraordinary outcomes.

This is what the book's title means. Five times your wealth in fourteen years is not a prediction. It is not a promise that requires the market to perform in a specific way. It is the mechanical outcome of a system that uses the structural advantages available to every Australian dual-income household - combined borrowing power, negative gearing, the CGT discount, franking credits, new-build depreciation, deductible investment debt, and the offset account - to compound wealth at a rate that no single asset class, no single strategy, and no single decision can match.

The Australian tax system is the silent partner in both paths. It returned tens of thousands of dollars each year through PAYG variations, franking credits, depreciation deductions, and negative gearing. That money, reinvested instead of consumed, was the difference between 3X and 5X. The couple who spends the tax refund has a good portfolio. The couple who reinvests it has a wealth-building engine.

And both couples - whether they own a home or rent one, whether they recycle debt or use margin, whether they start with $200,000 or $1 million - are running the same system. Two engines. One process. Time.

The system does not care which path you take. It cares whether you show up. Year after year. Contribution after contribution. Top-up after top-up. The couple who follows the process does not need to be right about the future. They need to be consistent in the present. And consistency, compounded across fourteen years, is worth more than any prediction ever made.

*Important: the figures in this chapter are illustrative projections based on historical long-term Australian market averages. They are not predictions of future returns and do not constitute personal financial advice. Actual outcomes will vary depending on market conditions, individual tax circumstances, lending availability, household discipline, and the specific structure implemented. Before adopting any strategy described here, consult a licensed financial adviser who can model the framework against your specific position.

WEALTH BUILDER REFLECTION

One question to sit with:
We have read the two paths. We have seen the numbers. Now - which path is ours? And what is the first move we can make, this month, to start the process?

One truth to keep:
The couple who follows a process does not need to predict the future. They need to show up. And showing up, consistently, across fourteen years, is a strategy that has not failed.

Scan to access your free 14-Year Bricks & Stocks Tracker - built for the blueprint in this chapter.

THE NUMBER THAT CHANGES EVERYTHING

Here is the question the investible scoreboard quietly ignores: where does each couple live, and what does it cost them?

Hugh and Sana own their home. Across these fourteen years, it has done what their investment property did - grown at roughly 5 per cent a year, climbing from $1.75 million to approximately $3.46 million. After the mortgage, their equity in it is close to $2 million. That equity is real wealth, and it sits entirely outside the 5.4X investible figure. It was never counted.

Luca and Dani own no home. For fourteen years they paid rent - starting near $61,000 a year and rising with the market- more than $1.2 million handed to a landlord over the period. That money bought them shelter and nothing else. No equity. No asset at the end. Gone.

Now put both couples on the same footing. The homeowner has an occupancy cost too: the interest on the portion of their loan that funds the home they live in - roughly $630,000 across fourteen years, on a balance that steadily falls as they pay it down. Compare that, like for like, to the renter's $1.2 million in rent. The renter pays nearly twice as much to occupy a home, and owns nothing at the end. The homeowner pays less, and owns a $3.46 million house.

Add it all together - investments, home equity, and the true cost of having somewhere to live - and the picture inverts:

On investments alone, the renter finishes ahead: 6.8X to 5.4X. But once the home is counted, the homeowner's $500,000 has become 8.15X in total wealth - and they finish nearly $1.9 million ahead. The home is the difference.

This is not an argument that renting is a mistake. Luca and Dani built genuine wealth - more of it, in pure investment terms, than Hugh and Sana did. The margin strategy worked exactly as designed. But the couple who can run the system and own the roof over their head holds an advantage that no investment multiple captures: a large, appreciating, leveraged asset they were always going to need anyway, because everyone has to live somewhere. The rent you do not pay is a return. The home you own while you invest is a second engine running quietly alongside the first.

Both paths clear 5X. Both prove the system. But the full picture - the one the appendix lays out in detail - is that owning your home is not a competing use of money. It is the foundation that makes everything else compound harder.

The next chapter does not add another strategy. It does not introduce another couple or another set of numbers. It asks the question that has been sitting quietly beneath every chapter in this book: ***what kind of wealth builders do you want to be?*** *The answer is not financial. It is personal. And it is the thing that will still be true long after the last dividend lands and the last top-up is drawn.*

CHAPTER 13

What Kind of Wealth Builders Do You Want to Be?

Behaviour beats intelligence

Remember Amy and Will from the very first chapter? When we met them, they had had a "kitchen table scare", but three years later, they had bought a unit in Woodville - a two-bedroom place renting for $380 a week (cash flow neutral from the first month), and an ETF portfolio that was growing in the background.

Now, another four years have passed; it is a Saturday morning in Henley Beach, and Amy is watching her daughter build a sandcastle at the water's edge.

The girl is seven, and she has her mother's concentration. She works in silence, patting the wet sand into walls with both hands, digging a moat with a plastic spoon, frowning at a turret that keeps collapsing on one side. She does not ask for help. She adjusts and tries again. Amy watches this and feels something she cannot quite name - not pride exactly, though there is pride in it. Something closer to recognition.

Will is beside her on a towel. He was reading something on his phone a few minutes ago - not the portfolio, not the offset balance, just the news - and he put it down when the wind picked up. Their son is further out, knee-deep in the shallows, pretending to be a shark. A jogger passes behind them on the esplanade. The coffee from the kiosk on the corner is still warm.

Amy notices this. She notices it because there was a time, not so long ago, when Saturday mornings asked everything. When the mental arithmetic started before the coffee was made - the mortgage payment on Thursday, the car registration next month, the daycare fees that had gone up again, the feeling of being one unexpected bill away from something she didn't want to think about. Saturday mornings used to carry weight. This one doesn't. And the absence of that weight is so unfamiliar that she almost doesn't trust it.

They have been building for seven years now. Two properties. A share portfolio that runs on autopilot. Two super accounts that are, for the first time in their lives, doing what superannuation was always supposed to do. An offset account that holds enough to absorb any reasonable disruption without selling a thing.

Neither of them planned this moment. They didn't picture it in Year One, when the offset felt painfully slow, and the first investment property cost them sleep for a month. They didn't imagine it in Year Three, when interest rates rose, and the Woodville unit sat vacant, and Will wanted to sell everything and pay down the mortgage. They certainly didn't foresee it at the start, when Amy sat at the kitchen table with her laptop open, a six-month-old asleep in the next room, and spent twenty minutes choosing an ETF she wasn't sure was right.

The process was not exciting. It was not clever. It did not make them feel like financial geniuses. Most months it felt like nothing was happening at all.

But this morning - this ordinary Saturday morning, with sand between their toes and two kids who don't yet understand what money means - is what seven years of process looks like from the inside. It looks like not being afraid. It looks like watching a daughter build a sandcastle and not calculating what her school fees will cost next term. It looks like a kind of freedom that has nothing to do with the number in the account and everything to do with the structure underneath it.

Amy picks up a shell and turns it over in her hand.

"Do you remember the twenty minutes?" she says.

Will doesn't need to ask what she means. "The ETF."

"I thought I'd pick the wrong one."

"You picked it anyway."

She turns the shell over again. "That was it, wasn't it? That was the moment everything started."

Will doesn't answer, because they both already know. It wasn't a brilliant decision. It wasn't even a confident one. It was a scared woman at a kitchen table choosing to behave like someone who invests, before she felt like someone who invests. And then doing it again the next month. And the month after that.

The wealth they have built is not extraordinary by any measure. It will not make a newspaper. It will not be the subject of a podcast. But it is theirs, and it is durable, and it exists because two people decided - not once, but hundreds of times, in hundreds of small moments - to behave like the kind of people who build things that last.

That is what this book has been about. Not the property. Not the shares. Not the tax advantages or the super optimisation or the debt recycling. Those are the tools. The tools matter. But the tools are not the thing.

The thing is the behaviour.

WEALTH BUILDERS THROUGH TIME

The Wayfinders of the Pacific - Polynesia, 1500 BC-1200 AD

Between roughly 1500 BC and 1200 AD, the navigators of the Pacific - Polynesian, Melanesian, Micronesian - accomplished the largest oceanic expansion in human history. They settled every habitable island across the

Polynesian Triangle and beyond, from Tonga to Hawai'i, from Samoa to Aotearoa, from Fiji to Rapa Nui.

They did this without compasses. Without paper charts. Without metal tools or written language. The European navigators who would later cross the same waters required chronometers, sextants, printed star tables, and centuries of accumulated cartographic knowledge. The Pacific voyagers needed none of it.

What they had instead was behaviour.

The wayfinding families of the Pacific held a belief that the European world would not fully understand for another thousand years: that knowledge worth keeping must live in the body, not on the page. A star chart written on vellum can be lost in a storm. A navigation system encoded in years of practice, in the muscles and the memory and the daily habits of a trained navigator, cannot be taken from you.

They did not believe in intelligence as the deciding factor. The cleverest person in the village was not necessarily the one chosen to navigate. The one chosen was the one whose behaviour could be trusted across weeks of open ocean - patient under pressure, disciplined in observation, steady when the swells and the stars gave contradictory signals. Brilliance without composure was worthless at sea. Composure without brilliance could still find land.

Each generation of navigators made the same fundamental decision: to teach the system, not the shortcut. A young navigator did not learn to read a star by memorising its name. They learned by spending years observing - lying in the hull of the canoe at night, feeling the pattern of the swells against the wood, watching the movement of birds at dawn, the colour of the water as the depth changed, the shape of clouds forming above an island still below the horizon.

The knowledge was a system of habits, built through repetition and refined through correction. It could not be taught in a single lesson. It could not be passed on as a document. It could only be transmitted through sustained, disciplined, intergenerational practice - one navigator teaching the next, who taught the next, who taught the next, across centuries, until the system was older and more reliable than any individual who carried it.

The tension was not a single crisis but a permanent condition. Every voyage was a test - not of whether the navigator was clever enough, but of whether their behaviour would hold when the familiar signals disappeared. There were passages where the stars were obscured for days behind low cloud. Currents that shifted without warning. Moments when every instinct said to turn back, and only the discipline of the system - trust the swell pattern, count the days, watch the birds - kept the canoe on course.

The navigators who relied on intelligence alone - who improvised, who trusted their instincts over the system, who believed they could read the ocean better than the generations before them - were the ones who did not arrive. The ones who arrived were the ones whose behaviour had been trained so deeply that it functioned even when their confidence failed, especially when their confidence failed.

The result was the most remarkable sustained achievement in the history of oceanic exploration. Every major island group in the Pacific was discovered and settled - not by accident, not by luck, but by a system of behaviour passed from parent to child across hundreds of generations. The voyages were not one-off feats of courage. They were repeatable, reliable outcomes of a process that worked because it did not depend on any individual being brilliant. It depended on every individual being disciplined.

When European navigators finally reached the Pacific in the eighteenth century, they were astonished. Captain Cook's expedition encountered islanders thousands of kilometres from the nearest landmass who knew exactly where they were, where they had come from, and how to get back. The navigator Tupaia drew Cook a chart of some seventy islands he could locate without instruments, by reading the ocean itself. The Europeans had superior technology. The Pacific voyagers had superior behaviour. And across the span of three thousand years, behaviour had arrived first.

The wayfinders did not navigate by being smarter than the ocean. They navigated by building a system of behaviour so deep and so durable that it could survive anything the ocean threw at them. They understood something that sits at the heart of every chapter in this book: that intelligence gets you started, but behaviour gets you there. The family that builds habits - consistent, disciplined, passed from one generation to the next - will outperform the family that relies on being right.

An Australian couple in 2026 is not navigating the Pacific in a double-hulled canoe. But they are navigating something that feels, in its own way, just as vast - a financial landscape that shifts constantly, that rewards patience over prediction, and that cannot be mastered by intelligence alone. The couple who builds a system of behaviour - who shows up, follows the process, and passes that discipline to the next generation - will arrive. Not because they were clever. Because they were consistent.

A PRESENT-DAY STORY

The Couple Who Stopped Trying to Be Smart

Amy was a speech pathologist working three days a week at a community health centre in Glenelg. Will was a logistics coordinator at a freight company in Outer Harbour. Combined income around $155,000. When they first sat down together to talk seriously about money, their daughter was six months old and their finances looked like most young families in Adelaide's western suburbs - a mortgage on a three-bedroom house in Seaton, two super accounts neither of them had checked since changing jobs, a savings account with $11,000 in it, and a vague sense that they should be doing something more but no clear idea what.

They were not high earners. They were not behind. They had the kind of household income that feels like it should be enough but never quite is - enough to live on, not enough to build on. At least, that is what they believed.

Amy believed that building wealth required a level of financial sophistication she did not have. She had watched her father lose money on a managed fund in the early 2000s and concluded, reasonably, that investing was a game for people who understood things she didn't. She associated shares with risk and property with safety, and she assumed that both required more money than they had before either one could be useful.

Will's belief was different but led to the same place. He thought they needed to earn more before they could start. "We'll invest when there's enough left over," he said, more than once. There was never enough left over. There never is, for the couple who waits for surplus to appear on its own.

What shifted - slowly, over the course of a year - was not their knowledge. It was their identity. They stopped thinking of themselves as people who would invest one day and started behaving like people who invest now. The distinction sounds small. It was not. It was the most important thing that ever happened to their finances, and it had nothing to do with a product, a platform, or a tax strategy. It was a decision about who they were.

Their first decision was unglamorous. They moved $9,000 of their savings into an offset account linked to their mortgage. The interest saving was modest - roughly $40 a week. But the behaviour it required was the behaviour that mattered: looking at the mortgage not as a burden to endure but as a structure to use.

From there, they set up an automatic transfer of $400 a month into a low-cost diversified ETF through an online brokerage. Amy chose the fund. It took her twenty minutes. She would later say it was the most important twenty minutes of her financial life - not because the fund was perfect, but because the act of choosing broke something open. She was no longer someone who didn't invest. She was someone who did.

Over the following three years, the decisions accumulated. They consolidated their super into lower-fee indexed options. They bought a two-bedroom unit in Woodville - modest, tenanted, cash-flow neutral after tax - using equity from the Seaton house and a structure that kept their borrowing conservative and their buffer intact.

None of it was dramatic. None of it required special knowledge. Every single step was available to any couple with two incomes, a mortgage, and the willingness to follow a sequence.

The tension came in Year Three, when interest rates rose, and the Woodville unit sat vacant for six weeks between tenants. Will came home one evening with a spreadsheet he had built during his lunch break. It showed what would happen if they sold the unit, closed the share portfolio, and used the proceeds to pay down the mortgage.

"We'd be debt-free in eight years," he said. "No tenants. No market. No stress."

Amy looked at the spreadsheet. She understood the appeal. The number on the mortgage was the thing that kept Will up at night, and removing it felt like removing the anxiety itself.

"What happens to the super?" she asked.

He hadn't modelled that."What happens to the compounding on the shares?"

He hadn't modelled that either. "You're modelling the relief," Amy said. "Not the outcome."

It was the sharpest thing she had ever said about money. And it was not something she had read in a book or heard in a seminar. It was something she had learned by living inside the system long enough to understand what it was doing. The relief of eliminating debt was real. The cost of eliminating the assets that the debt was building was also real - and it was larger, and it was permanent, and Will's spreadsheet had not captured it because a spreadsheet cannot model the future you don't build.

Will closed the spreadsheet. They found a tenant the following week. The share portfolio, which had dropped fourteen per cent during the correction, recovered within nine months. The offset absorbed the vacancy without touching their living expenses.

The system held. Not because they were brave. Because the structure made stillness possible when everything inside them wanted to move.

Seven years after that first $9,000 went into the offset, Amy and Will owned their home with $127,000 in the offset and a mortgage that was shrinking faster than the original schedule. The Woodville unit had grown modestly in value and was returning steady rent. Their share portfolio had crossed $94,000 - built almost entirely from automatic contributions they no longer thought about. Both super accounts were consolidated, optimised, and growing at a rate that surprised them every time they checked.

They were seven years into a fourteen-year process, and the compounding was only now starting to show itself. The first four years had felt glacial. Year five had felt like treading water. Years six and seven had begun to move in a way that made both of them sit up. The curve was bending. Not because anything had changed in their behaviour - the contributions were the same, the process was the same - but because time was doing what time does when you give it a system to work with.

Their combined net position was not life-changing by the standards of a financial magazine. But it was life-changing by the standards of two people who, seven years earlier, had $11,000 in a savings account and no plan.

What changed was not their intelligence. Amy would be the first to tell you she still doesn't fully understand franking credits. Will still cannot explain how debt recycling works without drawing a diagram on a napkin. They are not financial experts. They are not even particularly confident about money.

What they are is consistent. They show up. They follow the process. They sit down together once a quarter and look at the numbers - not because they enjoy it, but because that is what the kind of people they have decided to be.

And here is the thing Amy noticed on the beach that Saturday morning, the thing that made her stop and pick up a shell and hold it in her hand for a long time before saying anything.

Her daughter has never seen her parents fight about money. Has never heard the phrase "we can't afford it" used as a weapon in a quiet kitchen. Has never felt the particular silence that descends on a household when the bills arrive and nobody wants to open them. The girl is seven. She builds sandcastles with total concentration and does not know that the ground beneath her is steady because two people spent seven years making it so.

That absence - the anxiety the daughter will never know was there - is not in the spreadsheet either. But it is the truest return on everything Amy and Will have built. And it is the one that will compound longest.

Amy and Will did not outthink the market. They did not time their entry into shares or predict the rate cycle or find a property that nobody else had noticed. They behaved. Consistently. Together. Across years that were sometimes exciting and mostly were not. The wealth they built is the direct, measurable product of behaviour - not brilliance, not luck, not a single inspired decision, but the accumulated weight of hundreds of ordinary ones.

That is what this book has been trying to show you, across twelve chapters and as many stories. The couples who build lasting wealth are not the smartest couples. They are the most consistent. And consistency is not a talent. It is a choice - made again and again, in the quiet moments when nobody is watching, and the headlines are saying something else.

You do not need to be smarter than the market. You need to behave better than the couple who is.

WEALTH BUILDER REFLECTION

One question to sit with:
What do you want to be true about how you and your partner handled money - not just the numbers, but the way you did it?

One truth to keep:
The couple who builds wealth through behaviour, not brilliance, will build something that outlasts them. That is the point. That has always been the point.

Scan here to join the 5X newsletter - one email when it matters, for the couple who's already building.

EPILOGUE

This book began at a kitchen table in Brisbane. Two people, a laptop open between them, the kids in bed. A spreadsheet that told a story neither of them wanted to read. And one sentence, spoken quietly into the silence of a Sunday night:

"We should be further ahead than this."

If you have read this far, you are not the same couple who opened this book. You may not feel different. The mortgage is still there. The super still feels abstract. The share market still moves in ways that make your stomach tighten. Saturday mornings still come with lists and logistics and the low hum of a life that never quite slows down.

But something has shifted. You know things now that you didn't know then. You know that two incomes is not just a lifestyle - it is a structural advantage most couples never use. You know that the offset account is not a savings vehicle - it is the load-bearing wall of the entire system. You know that shares are not gambling and property is not safety and superannuation is not something you deal with later. You know that the Australian tax system was built to reward exactly the kind of patient, disciplined, long-term building that this book describes.

And you know - because twelve chapters of stories have shown you, not told you - that the couples who built well were not the smartest, the highest-earning, or the luckiest. They were the ones who showed up. Who followed the process. Who sat across from each other at the kitchen table, looked at the numbers, and decided - together - to keep going.

That is the invitation this book leaves you with. Not to be brilliant. Not to time the market or find the perfect property or master the intricacies of franking credits. But to decide, as a couple, what kind of wealth builders you want to be. And then to behave accordingly. For a year. Then another. Then another after that.

The rest takes care of itself. It always has.

Two ordinary assets, patiently managed with discipline and structure, will outperform almost any clever strategy - across every era, every market, and every generation.

Now go build.

Appendix A - Field Notes

WHAT TO TAKE INTO THE FIELD

The teaching is done. What follows is the compressed version - what to check, and where to check it. Use it standing outside an open inspection, or on the evening you finally set up the automatic transfer.

A.1 Property - The Five Layers

Work from the broadest layer to the most specific. No single layer gives you the answer. Together they tell you whether a decision is structurally sound.

City & Region

Diversified economy, not dependent on a single industry. Employment trending up across more than one sector - healthcare, education, government, professional services, construction.

LGA websites for the economic profile, major employers, approved infrastructure. ABS for employment and unemployment by region.

Suburb

Sustained population growth rather than a spike. Proximity to expanding employment nodes. Healthy owner-occupier to investor ratio. Committed infrastructure - hospital upgrades, rail extensions, centre redevelopments.

realestate.com.au for growth and rental history. Cotality OnTheHouse for past sales and trends. SQM Research for yields and vacancy rates. Microburbs for liveability - some free data, the detailed analysis is paid.

Street & Pocket

Flood zones, bushfire overlays, flight paths, major road noise. The layer investors skip, and where the risk usually hides.

Council LGA flood maps, searchable by address. State planning authority for bushfire overlays. Stand on the street at different times of day. Ask the agent directly about known overlays.

Property & Block

Current zoning and any development applications lodged nearby. Comparable sales on the same street or pocket - your reality check on whether the price reflects the market or the vendor's ambition.

Council LGA website for zoning and DAs. Conveyancer for a title search and planning certificate. Sold data on realestate.com.au and Domain.

Condition

Pest and building inspection as the minimum. Roof audit and asbestos report on older stock. For units, the strata report - sinking fund, dispute history, planned maintenance, likelihood of special levies.

Licensed inspectors. Strata report before you commit. A ten-minute call to a local property manager will tell you what tenants in that area actually value.

No single source of truth. Check the data across more than one source before you build a decision on it.

A.2 Shares & ETFs - The Decision Filter

Four criteria. They have not changed in decades, and the list of funds that satisfy all four is short.

Breadth. An ETF that tracks a broad market index - not a sector or a theme. A single diversified fund holding Australian and international shares in one package is the simplest way to get it, and for many couples it is the entire portfolio.

Cost. Between 0.04 and 0.27 per cent a year for a broad index fund. Above 0.30 per cent is worth questioning. Above 0.50 per cent is a managed fund wearing an index fund's clothes.

Size. Above $500 million under management, ideally above $1 billion. Tighter tracking, lower spreads, near-zero chance of being wound up.

Simplicity. If you cannot say what the fund holds in one sentence, it is not the right fund for a long-term system. Complexity is almost always cost in disguise.

What to ignore

One-, three- and five-year past performance. Star ratings from research houses - they measure history, not future. Thematic funds, which ask you to predict which theme wins. Actively managed ETFs, which charge more for the stock-picking the index was meant to replace.

The structure

A low-cost Australian brokerage account. One or two broad funds. An automatic transfer each fortnight or month, at an amount the household can sustain without disturbing the mortgage or the offset. Dividends reinvested, or directed to the offset. Then leave it alone.

You are not trying to pick the winning ship. You are trying to own the fleet.

A.3 The Blended System - Your Annual Two-Engine Check

Once a year, across a week of appointments with the broker, the accountant and the adviser - not crammed into a single evening. Six questions.

Are both engines running - property and shares - or has one quietly stalled?

Has the home been revalued, and is there new equity available at 80 per cent LVR to draw down and deploy?

Is the offset account working as hard as the mortgage, and has this year's debt-recycling cycle been executed?

Have both super accounts been reviewed - allocation, insurance, contributions against the concessional cap?

Are both incomes being used deliberately across tax, borrowing and ownership - or is the structure one you inherited rather than chose?

Could you absorb a rate rise, a vacancy or a market correction without selling anything?

Two ordinary assets, patiently managed with discipline and structure, will outperform almost any clever strategy - across every era, every market, and every generation.

Appendix B - The Numbers Behind the Stories

WHERE EVERY FIGURE IN CHAPTER 12 COMES FROM

Chapter 12 tells the story. This is the mechanical companion - the deployment, the debt, the cash flow and the year-by-year position for both paths. Every figure traces to the same model. The appendix reconciles to the chapter; the chapter does not change to suit the appendix.

All figures are illustrative projections on the locked fourteen-year model at a 45 per cent marginal rate. They are not predictions, and they are not advice.

B.1 Where the $500,000 Goes

Both couples deploy the same capital. The difference is where it comes from - Hugh and Sana release equity from a home they own; Luca and Dani deploy savings they have accumulated while renting.

Capital deployment	Homeowner	Renter
Starting capital	$500,000	$500,000
Investment property deposit (20% of $1.25M)	($250,000)	($250,000)
Purchase costs - duty, conveyancing, inspections	($17,500)	($17,500)
Diversified share portfolio	($232,500)	($232,500)
TOTAL DEPLOYED	$500,000	$500,000

Homeowner capital is released from a $1.75M home against a $900,000 living loan. Renter capital is the couple's own savings - not borrowed.

Investment debt at the start

Debt	Homeowner	Renter
Investment property loan (80% LVR, interest-only)	$1,000,000	$1,000,000
Equity release against the home (deductible)	$500,000	-
Margin loan (opens at 22% LVR)	-	$65,577
TOTAL INVESTMENT DEBT	$1,500,000	$1,065,577

The renter starts with substantially less debt. The margin facility grows with the portfolio, topped up annually to hold roughly 22 per cent LVR, reaching about $724,000 by year fourteen.

B.2 Year One - What the System Costs to Run

The costs arrive monthly, before the tax system returns a cent. This is the year the couple feels it.

Year one cash flow	Homeowner	Renter
Investment property interest ($1M @ 6%)	($60,000)	($60,000)
Share-debt interest	($30,000)	($6,230)
Property running costs	($10,000)	($10,000)
Total cash out	($100,000)	($76,230)
Rent received (4% of $1.25M)	$50,000	$50,000
Dividends received	$4,650	$5,962
Tax benefit - negative gearing and franking	$31,899	$21,314
NET OUT-OF-POCKET COST	$18,101	$4,915
Covered by the annual contribution	$20,000	$20,000

Share-debt interest is the equity-release tranche at 6 per cent for the homeowner, and the margin loan at 9.5 per cent for the renter. Depreciation of $20,000 is claimed but is not a cash cost - it reaches the couple only through the tax benefit.

B.3 The Cash-Flow Rhythm

The question this answers is the one couples actually ask: when does the strategy stop costing money and start paying? The line below excludes the $20,000 contribution, so it measures whether the system funds itself.

Net cash flow before contribution	Homeowner	Renter
Year 1	($13,451)	$1,046
Year 4	$3,273	$17,256
Year 7	$19,096	$31,640
Year 14	$76,763	$90,086
CROSSOVER YEAR	Year 4	Year 1

The renter crosses earlier because they carry less debt. Their home rent - which grows every year and builds no asset - sits outside this table and is settled in B.5.

B.4 The Fourteen-Year Position

Both paths run the same two engines. Their balance sheets diverge because of how the share side is funded.

Position at year 14	Homeowner	Renter
Share portfolio	$2,165,758	$2,661,017
Less: share debt	($920,000)	($724,159)
Net share equity	$1,245,758	$1,936,858
Investment property value	$2,474,914	$2,474,914
Less: investment property loan	($1,000,000)	($1,000,000)
Investment property equity	$1,474,914	$1,474,914
NET INVESTIBLE POSITION	$2,720,673	$3,411,773
MULTIPLE OF $500,000	5.44X	6.82X

B.5 True Wealth - Like for Like

The renter's investible multiple is higher. That is not the whole picture, because the two couples do not pay the same price to live somewhere. A fair comparison has to count the home and the cost of occupying it.

True net wealth at year 14	Homeowner	Renter
Net investible position	$2,720,673	$3,411,773
Plus: home equity	$1,985,539	-
Less: living-loan interest over 14 years	($633,525)	-
Less: rent paid over 14 years	-	($1,200,416)
TRUE NET WEALTH	$4,072,686	$2,211,357
MULTIPLE OF $500,000	8.15X	4.42X

Home value of $3,464,880 at year 14 ($1.75M growing at 5%), less a living loan paid down to $559,341. Rent assumes a 3.5 per cent yield on an equivalent $1.75M home, growing at 5 per cent.

The homeowner finishes $1,861,330 ahead. The difference is not investment skill - both couples run the same system with the same discipline. It is occupancy cost. The homeowner pays $633,525 in interest and keeps a $3.5 million asset. The renter pays $1,200,416 and keeps nothing. The lesson is not that owning beats investing. It is that the two decisions are separate, and both have to be made deliberately.

B.6 Rate Sensitivity

Every scenario re-runs the full fourteen-year model at the stated mortgage rate, held constant for the whole term.

Scenario	Rate	Homeowner	Renter
Rates fall 1%	5.0%	5.98X	7.27X
Rates fall 0.5%	5.5%	5.69X	7.04X

Scenario	Rate	Homeowner	Renter
THIS BLUEPRINT (BASE)	6.0%	5.44X	6.82X
Rates rise 0.5%	6.5%	5.31X	6.61X
Rates rise 1%	7.0%	5.25X	6.39X
Rates rise 2%	8.0%	5.21X	5.98X
Rates rise 3%	9.0%	5.20X	5.60X
Rates rise 4%	10.0%	5.19X	5.56X

The homeowner is more rate-sensitive - total investment debt reaches $1.92 million against the renter's $1.72 million. Both paths hold above 5X even under a four-point rise, because over half the final position is property equity that keeps growing regardless of borrowing costs. These projections hold both the rate and asset growth constant.

B.7 The Historical Test

Projections are assumptions. This runs the same fourteen-year model through real Australian market data across two contrasting windows - one share-poor, one share-strong.

Window	Shares p.a.	Property p.a.	Homeowner	Renter
1998–2011 - dot-com crash and GFC	5.1%	8.2%	5.78X	7.20X
2012–2025 - the most recent fourteen years	14.4%	5.3%	7.06X	8.92X

Shares are a 60/40 blend of MSCI World ex-Australia (AUD) and the ASX 200 Accumulation Index. Property is the ABS Residential Property Price Index across eight capital cities. Sources appear in the References under Chapter 12.

The first window is the one that matters. Shares returned an average of 5.1 per cent a year across fourteen years containing two major crashes - and both paths still cleared 5X, because the property engine and the reinvested tax benefits carried the system while the share engine stalled. The second window shows what the same discipline produces when shares run hot. Neither result requires a forecast. Both require both engines running.

A note on timing. Outcomes depend on when a fourteen-year run begins. A start immediately before a crash - 2005 or 2007, for instance - produces a weaker result, because borrowed equity is fully deployed just as the market falls. Runs beginning after a crash fare better. This is the timing risk the chapter names, and no model removes it.

-·-

All figures in this appendix are illustrative projections on the locked fourteen-year model, not predictions of future returns. The author is a licensed financial adviser, but this book is general in nature and does not constitute personal advice. Consult a licensed adviser before acting on anything described here.

B.8 The Year-by-Year Grid

THE WHOLE FOURTEEN YEARS, ONE PAGE EACH

The tables above give the beginning and the end. These give every year in between - the same figures the model produces, so any line in Chapter 12 can be traced to the year it came from. All figures are in thousands of dollars unless marked otherwise.

Path 1 - Hugh & Sana (homeowner)

Year	1	2	3	4	5	6	7	8	9	10	11	12	13	14
Share portfolio	246	451	661	758	881	969	1,067	1,176	1,298	1,435	1,589	1,760	1,952	2,166
Less: share debt	(500)	(677)	(842)	(872)	(920)	(920)	(920)	(920)	(920)	(920)	(920)	(920)	(920)	(920)
Net share equity	(254)	(226)	(181)	(114)	(39)	49	147	256	378	515	669	840	1,032	1,246
Investment property	1,312	1,378	1,447	1,519	1,595	1,675	1,759	1,847	1,939	2,036	2,138	2,245	2,357	2,475
Less: IP loan	(1,000)	(1,000)	(1,000)	(1,000)	(1,000)	(1,000)	(1,000)	(1,000)	(1,000)	(1,000)	(1,000)	(1,000)	(1,000)	(1,000)
IP equity	312	378	447	519	595	675	759	847	939	1,036	1,138	1,245	1,357	1,475
Home equity	454	386	335	425	504	637	778	925	1,080	1,243	1,415	1,596	1,786	1,986
Total investment debt	1,500	1,677	1,842	1,872	1,920	1,920	1,920	1,920	1,920	1,920	1,920	1,920	1,920	1,920
Out-of-pocket cost	18	16	20	23	22	22	20	18	15	13	10	7	4	1
NET INVESTIBLE	**59**	**152**	**267**	**405**	**557**	**725**	**906**	**1,103**	**1,317**	**1,552**	**1,807**	**2,085**	**2,389**	**2,721**
MULTIPLE	**0.12**	**0.30**	**0.53**	**0.81**	**1.11**	**1.45**	**1.81**	**2.21**	**2.63**	**3.10**	**3.61**	**4.17**	**4.78**	**5.44**

Share debt rises from $500,000 to $920,000 as home equity is released and recycled, then holds once the responsible-lending ceiling is reached. Home equity is shown for context; it sits outside the investible multiple and is settled in B.5.

Path 2 - Luca & Dani (renter)

Year	1	2	3	4	5	6	7	8	9	10	11	12	13	14
Share portfolio	328	419	506	600	707	829	969	1,128	1,309	1,515	1,750	2,016	2,318	2,661
Less: margin debt	(66)	(107)	(135)	(162)	(191)	(225)	(263)	(306)	(355)	(412)	(475)	(548)	(631)	(724)
Net share equity	262	312	371	439	516	605	706	822	954	1,104	1,274	1,468	1,688	1,937
Investment property	1,312	1,378	1,447	1,519	1,595	1,675	1,759	1,847	1,939	2,036	2,138	2,245	2,357	2,475
Less: IP loan	(1,000)	(1,000)	(1,000)	(1,000)	(1,000)	(1,000)	(1,000)	(1,000)	(1,000)	(1,000)	(1,000)	(1,000)	(1,000)	(1,000)
IP equity	312	378	447	519	595	675	759	847	939	1,036	1,138	1,245	1,357	1,475
Margin top-up	-	41	28	27	29	33	38	43	49	56	64	73	82	94
Out-of-pocket cost	5	3	3	3	2	2	2	1	1	1	1	1	2	3
NET INVESTIBLE	**575**	**690**	**818**	**958**	**1,111**	**1,280**	**1,465**	**1,669**	**1,893**	**2,140**	**2,412**	**2,713**	**3,045**	**3,412**
MULTIPLE	**1.15**	**1.38**	**1.64**	**1.92**	**2.22**	**2.56**	**2.93**	**3.34**	**3.79**	**4.28**	**4.82**	**5.43**	**6.09**	**6.82**

The margin facility is topped up each year to hold roughly 22 per cent LVR - the top-up row shows how much is drawn. Rent paid is not shown here; it is an occupancy cost, not an investment cost, and is settled in B.5.

Glossary

THE WORDS, IN PLAIN ENGLISH

You don't need any of these definitions to understand the stories in this book - the stories explain themselves. This is here for the moment you're standing in front of a banker, an accountant, or a contract, and you want the plain version of a word someone just used as if you already knew it. The page numbers point to where each idea is explained in the book. Rules and figures behind some of these terms change; the meanings don't.

Buffer · pp. 131–136, 171–174, 194 - The cash you deliberately hold back so that a rate rise, a vacancy or a lost income does not force a decision. Standard advice is three to six months of costs; the approach in this book is six to twelve - covering the home loan and core living expenses, because the investment property services itself through rent.

Capital gain · pp. 34–35, 88–89 - The profit when you sell an asset for more than you paid for it. The gain is only "realised" - and only taxed - when you actually sell. While you hold, a rise in value is just paper.

Capital gains tax (CGT) · pp. 34–35, 88–90 - The tax you pay on a realised capital gain. In Australia it isn't a separate tax with its own rate - the gain is added to your income for the year and taxed at your marginal rate.

CGT discount · pp. 34–35, 88–90 - A reduction in the taxable portion of a capital gain for individuals who have held an asset for more than twelve months. For most of the period this book describes, that discount has been 50 per cent. Time, quite literally, is rewarded by law. (The method is subject to change - confirm the current rule before you sell.)

Capital growth · pp. 41, 121, 133 - The increase in an asset's value over time, as distinct from the income it pays you along the way. Property and shares can deliver both; the balance between them is a choice, not an accident.

Compounding · pp. 17, 44, 117, 206 - Growth earning growth. When the returns on an investment are themselves reinvested and then earn returns of their own, the curve stops being a straight line and starts to bend upward. Time is the ingredient most people underestimate.

Concessional contributions · pp. 154–155 - Money paid into superannuation from pre-tax income - employer contributions and salary sacrifice - taxed at a lower rate inside super than most people's marginal rate. Limited each year by a cap set by the ATO.

Cross-collateralisation · pp. 68, 70, 74 - Using more than one property as security for the same loan. It suits the lender and quietly costs you options - selling or refinancing one property becomes a conversation about all of them. Worth avoiding unless there is a specific reason not to.

Debt recycling · pp. 146–151, 174 - Gradually replacing non-deductible debt (such as your home loan) with deductible debt used to buy income-producing investments. Done carefully, it turns the interest you were already paying into a tax-deductible expense while you build an investment portfolio.

Depreciation · pp. 51–52, 205 - A deduction for the decline in value of a building and the assets inside it. You claim it without spending a dollar in the year you claim it, which is why it is called a non-cash deduction - and why a depreciation schedule usually pays for itself in the first year.

Diversification · pp. 28, 117, 143–145 - Not putting everything in one place. Spreading money across different assets - here, property and shares - so that a bad year for one is not a bad year for everything you own.

Dividend · pp. 120–122, 147–149 - A share of a company's profits paid out to its shareholders, usually a few times a year. The income engine of share investing, as rent is the income engine of property.

Dollar-cost averaging · pp. 199, 203, 209 - Investing a fixed amount at regular intervals regardless of the price on the day. You buy more units when prices are low and fewer when they're high, which removes the impossible job of timing the market.

Equity · pp. 47, 66, 146–147, 198, 201–202 - The part of an asset you actually own - its value minus the debt against it. As you pay down a loan and the asset grows, your equity grows on both sides, and that equity can be borrowed against to build the next step.

ETF (exchange-traded fund) · pp. 113, 116–118, 125 - A single investment, traded on the share market like a share, that holds a basket of many underlying assets - often an entire index. One purchase, broad diversification, typically low fees.

Franking credit · pp. 120–121, 187–188 - A credit attached to an Australian dividend for the tax the company has already paid on its profits. It stops the same dollar being taxed twice and can reduce - sometimes refund - tax for the shareholder. A genuinely Australian advantage.

Gearing · pp. 52, 100–102 - Borrowing to invest. "Positively geared" means the investment's income covers its costs; "negatively geared" means it doesn't, and the shortfall is carried in the expectation of capital growth.

Interest-only loan · pp. 68, 74, 99, 168–170 - A loan on which you pay only the interest for a set period, leaving the balance untouched. It lifts cash flow in the short term and defers the repayment of principal - useful on investment debt, expensive if it becomes a habit.

Loan-to-value ratio (LVR) · pp. 151, 153, 209 - The size of a loan as a percentage of the value of the asset securing it. A $400,000 loan against a $500,000 property is an 80 per cent LVR. Lenders watch it closely; so should you.

Margin loan · pp. 129, 151–156, 209–212 - A loan used to buy shares, secured against the shares themselves. If their value falls far enough, the lender can issue a margin call - a demand to top up the loan or sell - which is why the buffer matters more than the opportunity.

Marginal tax rate · pp. 120–121 - The rate of tax you pay on your next dollar of income - the top band your income reaches. It's the number that makes deductions, gearing and which partner holds an asset actually matter for a couple.

Negative gearing · pp. 52, 100–102 - When the costs of an investment (including loan interest) exceed the income it produces, and that loss is offset against your other taxable income. One of the most powerful wealth tools available anywhere - and routinely misunderstood as something only the wealthy use.

Offset account · pp. 67–74, 96–99, 131–135 - A transaction account linked to your home loan. Every dollar sitting in it reduces the loan balance on which interest is charged, while remaining fully available to you. A uniquely useful Australian mortgage tool - liquidity and interest saving at the same time.

PAYG · p. 149 - Pay As You Go - the system by which tax is withheld from your wages each pay. It can be adjusted (via a PAYG withholding variation) so the benefit of a deduction reaches you through the year rather than as a lump sum at tax time.

Principal and interest (P&I) · pp. 66, 96–98 - The standard loan repayment - part interest, part debt reduction. Every payment leaves you owning slightly more of the asset outright. The opposite of interest-only, and the sensible default for the debt you are not deducting.

Redraw · pp. 72, 168, 170 - The ability to pull back extra repayments you have already made on a loan. It looks like an offset account and behaves differently for tax - redrawing for a private purpose can change the deductibility of the whole debt. Ask before you use it.

Rental yield · pp. 41–42, 84–85 - The annual rent on a property as a percentage of its value. A quick read on how hard the asset works for income, before you weigh it against its prospects for growth.

Serviceability · pp. 31, 73 - A lender's assessment of whether you can comfortably meet repayments - the gatekeeper to borrowing. For a couple, two incomes assessed together is the structural edge that single borrowers don't have.

Stamp duty · pp. 90, 199, 208 - The state tax paid when property changes hands, calculated on the purchase price. It is the largest of the upfront costs, and none of it is recoverable - one reason the transaction you don't make is sometimes the profitable one.

Superannuation · pp. 154–155 - Australia's compulsory long-term retirement savings system, taxed concessionally to encourage you to leave it alone. For a couple it means two accounts, two caps and two long-term compounding engines - most couples ignore it entirely until it's late.

Vacancy rate · pp. 84–85, 172 - The share of rental properties in an area sitting empty. A low, stable vacancy rate signals steady demand; a rising one is a quiet warning. A signal worth checking across more than one source.

Know the words, and the conversation stops happening to you.

References & Further Reading

THE SOURCES BEHIND THE STORIES

This book is built on stories, but the principles and the data behind them are real. The works below are grouped by chapter - the Australian sources used for the figures, and the histories worth reading if a particular story stayed with you. None of the organisations listed has reviewed or endorsed this book.

Introduction - The Fuggers of Augsburg (1480–1560)

- Steinmetz, Greg. The Richest Man Who Ever Lived: The Life and Times of Jakob Fugger. Simon & Schuster, 2015.
- Häberlein, Mark. The Fuggers of Augsburg: Pursuing Wealth and Honor in Renaissance Germany. University of Virginia Press, 2012.
- ASIC's MoneySmart. "Diversification." moneysmart.gov.au/how-to-invest/diversification. Accessed 7 July 2026.
- Australian Taxation Office. Capital Gains Tax Overview. ato.gov.au. Accessed 7 July 2026.
- Piketty, Thomas. Capital in the Twenty-First Century. Harvard University Press, 2014. [The r > g frame for long-run wealth accumulation.]

Chapter 1 - The Two-Engine System (Brendan and Kirra)

- Australian Bureau of Statistics. Household Income and Wealth, Australia (biennial). abs.gov.au. Accessed 7 July 2026.
- Reserve Bank of Australia. Submission to the Inquiry into Home Ownership (2015). rba.gov.au. Accessed 7 July 2026.
- Roberts, Stephen H. The Squatting Age in Australia 1835–1847. Melbourne University Press, 1935.
- Productivity Commission. Wealth Transfers and Their Economic Effects (2021). pc.gov.au. Accessed 7 July 2026.

- Jordà, Òscar; Knoll, Katharina; Kuvshinov, Dmitry; Schularick, Moritz; & Taylor, Alan M. "The Rate of Return on Everything, 1870–2015." The Quarterly Journal of Economics, 2019. [Long-run housing vs equity returns across 16 economies - the empirical backbone of the two-engine thesis; also underpins Chapters 7 and 12.]
- HILDA Survey - Household, Income and Labour Dynamics in Australia. Melbourne Institute of Applied Economic and Social Research. melbourneinstitute.unimelb.edu.au. Accessed 7 July 2026.

Chapter 2 - Choosing the First Property (Danielle and Matt)

- Cotality (formerly CoreLogic). Home Value Index - Monthly Indices Report. cotality.com. Accessed 7 July 2026.
- SQM Research. Vacancy Rates and Asking Rents Report. sqmresearch.com.au. Accessed 7 July 2026.
- Australian Bureau of Statistics. Residential Property Price Indexes: Eight Capital Cities. abs.gov.au. Accessed 7 July 2026.
- realestate.com.au - market insights and suburb data. realestate.com.au. Accessed 7 July 2026.
- Domain Group. Quarterly House Price Report. domain.com.au. Accessed 7 July 2026.
- Australian Housing and Urban Research Institute (AHURI). Housing research and policy evidence. ahuri.edu.au. Accessed 7 July 2026.

Chapter 3 - Property Cycles & Patience (Adam and Emily; Vaucluse / Marrickville)

- Stapledon, Nigel. Long-Term Housing Prices in Australia and Some Economic Perspectives (UNSW thesis and subsequent papers).
- Reserve Bank of Australia. A Century of House Prices in Australia - Discussion Paper (RDP). rba.gov.au. Accessed 7 July 2026.
- Lack, John & Templeton, Jacqueline. Sources of Australian Immigration History. University of Melbourne, 1988.
- Productivity Commission. Migration & Population Growth (various). pc.gov.au. Accessed 7 July 2026.

Chapter 4 - Funding the First Property (Mei and Chris)

- Australian Prudential Regulation Authority. ADI Statistics - Property Exposures. apra.gov.au. Accessed 7 July 2026.
- ASIC MoneySmart. "Interest-only home loans." moneysmart.gov.au. Accessed 7 July 2026.
- Reserve Bank of Australia. Statement on Monetary Policy - housing finance chapters (quarterly). rba.gov.au. Accessed 7 July 2026.
- Trocki, Carl A. Opium and Empire: Chinese Society in Colonial Singapore, 1800–1910. Cornell University Press, 1990.

Chapter 5 - Property Cycles in Action (Brisbane, 2020+)

- Cotality (formerly CoreLogic). Best of the Best Report (annual). cotality.com. Accessed 7 July 2026.
- Reserve Bank of Australia. Bulletin - regional housing markets and interstate migration during COVID. rba.gov.au. Accessed 7 July 2026.
- Australian Bureau of Statistics. Regional Population, Australia - interstate migration data (annual). abs.gov.au. Accessed 7 July 2026.
- KPMG. Australian Property Investor Outlook (annual).
- Cannon, Michael. The Land Boomers. Melbourne University Press, 1966.

Chapter 6 - The Australian Tax System for Property (Lachlan and Rebecca; Olivia and Nav)

- Australian Taxation Office. Rental Properties Guide (annual). ato.gov.au. Accessed 7 July 2026.
- Australian Taxation Office. Capital Gains Tax - Discount Method. ato.gov.au. Accessed 7 July 2026.
- Treasury. Tax Expenditures and Insights Statement (annual). treasury.gov.au. Accessed 7 July 2026.
- Productivity Commission. Housing Affordability and Supply (multiple reports).
- May 2026 Federal Budget - Budget Paper No. 2: Revenue Measures (negative gearing and CGT reforms). budget.gov.au. Accessed 7 July 2026.
- Walvin, James. The Quakers: Money and Morals. John Murray, 1997.

- Grattan Institute. Housing affordability, negative gearing and capital gains tax analysis. grattan.edu.au. Accessed 7 July 2026.

Chapter 7 - Shares as the Second Engine (Tom and Erin; Rachel and Dev)

- Vanguard Investments Australia. Index Chart (annual). vanguard.com.au. Accessed 7 July 2026.
- BetaShares. Australian ETF Review (annual). betashares.com.au. Accessed 7 July 2026.
- ASX. Australian Investor Study (biennial). asx.com.au. Accessed 7 July 2026.
- Bogle, John C. The Little Book of Common Sense Investing. Wiley, 2017.
- Malkiel, Burton G. A Random Walk Down Wall Street. W. W. Norton, 12th edition, 2019.
- Petram, Lodewijk. The World's First Stock Exchange. Columbia Business School Publishing, 2014.
- De Vries, Jan, & Ad van der Woude. The First Modern Economy: Success, Failure, and Perseverance of the Dutch Economy, 1500–1815. Cambridge University Press, 1997.
- S&P Dow Jones Indices. SPIVA Australia Scorecard (semi-annual). spglobal.com/spdji [Active vs passive performance - the evidence base for index investing.] Accessed 7 July 2026.

Chapter 8 - Behaviour in Downturns (Ravi and Jen; May 2022)

- Reserve Bank of Australia. Statement on Monetary Policy - May 2022. rba.gov.au. Accessed 7 July 2026.
- Reserve Bank of Australia. Cash Rate Target - Historical Series. rba.gov.au. Accessed 7 July 2026.
- Housel, Morgan. The Psychology of Money. Harriman House, 2020.
- Kahneman, Daniel. Thinking, Fast and Slow. Farrar, Straus and Giroux, 2011.
- Brady Commission. Report of the Presidential Task Force on Market Mechanisms. U.S. Government, January 1988.
- Australian Securities Exchange. 1987 Market Crash Archives. asx.com.au. Accessed 7 July 2026.

- Barber, Brad M., & Terrance Odean. "Trading Is Hazardous to Your Wealth: The Common Stock Investment Performance of Individual Investors." The Journal of Finance, 2000. [Overtrading and individual-investor underperformance.]

Chapter 9 - Smart Debt: Debt Recycling and Margin Lending (Craig and Tess; Nick and Jordan)

- Australian Taxation Office. Deductibility of Interest on Investment Loans - Taxation Ruling TR 2004/4. ato.gov.au. Accessed 7 July 2026.
- Australian Taxation Office. Margin Lending: Tax Treatment of Interest. ato.gov.au. Accessed 7 July 2026.
- ASIC MoneySmart. "Margin loans" and "Borrowing to invest." moneysmart.gov.au. Accessed 7 July 2026.
- Newlands, John. Put Not Your Trust in Money: A History of the Investment Trust Industry from 1868 to the Present Day. Chappin Kavanagh, 1997.
- Devine, T. M. The Scottish Nation: A Modern History. Penguin, 2012.
- Robert Fleming & Co. - historical archives via asset-management firms.

Chapter 10 - Layering the System (Deepa and Arun; Cameron and Jess)

- Reserve Bank of Australia. Submission to the Inquiry into the Future of Australia's Pension System. rba.gov.au. Accessed 7 July 2026.
- Australian Prudential Regulation Authority. Annual Superannuation Bulletin. apra.gov.au. Accessed 7 July 2026.
- Treasury. Retirement Income Review - Final Report (2020). treasury.gov.au. Accessed 7 July 2026.
- Cheng Lim-Keak. Social Change and the Chinese in Singapore. Singapore University Press, 1985.
- Trocki, Carl A. Singapore: Wealth, Power and the Culture of Control. Routledge, 2006.
- Grattan Institute. Money in Retirement: More Than Enough (2020). grattan.edu.au. Accessed 7 July 2026.
- Association of Superannuation Funds of Australia (ASFA). ASFA Retirement Standard. superannuation.asn.au. Accessed 7 July 2026.

Chapter 11 - Debt Management Across Two Incomes (Patrick and Tina)

- Australian Taxation Office. Marginal Tax Rates and Tax Brackets. ato.gov.au. Accessed 7 July 2026.
- ASIC MoneySmart. "Debt strategies" suite. moneysmart.gov.au. Accessed 7 July 2026.
- Treasury. Stage 3 Personal Income Tax Cuts - Budget Papers. treasury.gov.au. Accessed 7 July 2026.
- Wakita, Osamu. "The Emergence of the State in Sixteenth-Century Japan." Journal of Japanese Studies, 1982.
- Hayami, Akira & Miyamoto, Matao (eds.). Economic History of Japan. Oxford University Press, 2004.
- Schaede, Ulrike. "Forwards and Futures in Tokugawa-Period Japan." Journal of Banking & Finance, 1989.

Chapter 12 - The 14-Year Blueprint (Hugh and Sana; Luca and Dani)

- Australian Taxation Office. Negative Gearing and Rental Property Deductions. ato.gov.au. Accessed 7 July 2026.
- Australian Taxation Office. Depreciation and Capital Allowances - Division 43 (Capital Works) and Division 40 (Plant and Equipment). ato.gov.au. Accessed 7 July 2026.
- ASIC. Regulatory Guide 234: Advertising Financial Products. asic.gov.au. Accessed 7 July 2026.
- Vanguard Investments Australia. Australian Index Chart (annual) - long-run nominal share return assumption. vanguard.com.au. Accessed 7 July 2026.
- Reserve Bank of Australia. Historical Cash Rate Series. rba.gov.au. Accessed 7 July 2026.
- See also the Tracker Workbook and Appendix Year-by-Year Worksheet (companion materials to this chapter).

Conclusion - Wayfinders of the Pacific (1500 BC – 1280 AD)

- Lewis, David. We, the Navigators: The Ancient Art of Landfinding in the Pacific. University of Hawaii Press, 2nd edition, 1994.
- Finney, Ben. Voyage of Rediscovery: A Cultural Odyssey through Polynesia. University of California Press, 1994.
- Kirch, Patrick V. On the Road of the Winds: An Archaeological History of the Pacific Islands. University of California Press, revised edition, 2017.
- Howe, K. R. (ed.). Vaka Moana: Voyages of the Ancestors. University of Hawaii Press, 2007.
- Druett, Joan. Tupaia: Captain Cook's Polynesian Navigator. Praeger, 2011.
- Beaglehole, J. C. (ed.). The Journals of Captain James Cook. Hakluyt Society (multi-volume edition).

Cross-cutting Australian sources used throughout

- Australian Bureau of Statistics (abs.gov.au), Reserve Bank of Australia (rba.gov.au), Australian Taxation Office (ato.gov.au), ASIC's MoneySmart (moneysmart.gov.au), Treasury including Budget Papers and the Tax Expenditures Statement (treasury.gov.au), Australian Prudential Regulation Authority (apra.gov.au), and the Productivity Commission (pc.gov.au). Accessed 7 July 2026.

A note on methodology

All Australian financial data quoted in this book references publicly available sources current at the time of writing, in early 2026. Where the book makes projections or applies illustrative assumptions - particularly the worked examples in Chapter 12 and the accompanying appendix and tracker - those are illustrative projections only, not predictions of future returns. The author is a licensed financial planner, but this book is general in nature and does not constitute personal advice. Before adopting any strategy described here, consult a licensed financial adviser.

No single source of truth. Check the data across more than one source before you build a decision on it.

Acknowledgements

This book was written in the margins of a full life, and it could not have been written alone.

My deepest thanks go to my family, who supported me without reservation as I reached for my full potential - and who carried the early mornings and the lost weekends it took to get these words onto the page. Everything I build, I build with you in mind.

To my team, who made room for this. Thank you for giving me the time to write when there was always other work to be done, and for holding things steady while I did.

To my friends, who kept showing up even as I disappeared to my desk, typing away for far longer than I ever promised. Thank you for your patience, and for your good humour about it.

And above all, to my clients. Over the past twelve years you have given me the privilege of a front-row seat to your decisions - the setbacks, the courage, and the quiet, compounding wins. You gave me the confidence to write this book, because with you I have watched these principles actually work: patiently, through booms and corrections, in real homes and real portfolios. This book is the distillation of what you taught me, and I hope it honours the trust you placed in me.

Wealth is a shared project. So, it turns out, is writing about it.

About the Author

Victor Owi Idoko is a financial adviser with more than twelve years' experience helping Australian households turn income into lasting wealth. He holds the Chartered Financial Analyst (CFA) and Certified Financial Planner (CFP) designations, is an SMSF Specialist Advisor (SSA), and holds a Master of Commerce (M.Com).

Through his practice at CFV Advisory in Sydney, Victor has sat across the table from couples at the moments that quietly decide a financial life - the first investment property, the share portfolio started or stalled, the rate rise that tested a plan, the inheritance that could have been spent and wasn't. 5X Your Wealth grew directly out of that work: more than a decade of watching, up close, what separates the households that build steadily from those that don't.

His central conviction runs through every page - that in Australia the couple, not the individual, is the natural unit of wealth-building, and that most couples dramatically underuse the structural advantages they already hold. He fell into financial advice almost by accident, and stayed once he saw what it could do for people. Investing is the part he loves; financial planning is the whole package. Every qualification he has chased since - the CFA, the CFP, the SMSF specialist accreditation, the Master of Commerce - has served one aim: to be the best he can be for his clients, his team, his family, and himself.

Victor lives in Sydney. He hasn't started a family yet - though he hopes to, ideally with four children, if a future partner likes the idea. Away from the desk you'll find him training, giving time to his community, and forever taking on something hard for the joy of it: chess and piano, pottery and yoga, travel and writing, and a stubborn campaign to learn French. After all these years, he remains quietly obsessed with the same two ordinary assets this book is built on.

To keep building together - newsletter, tools, and a community of couples doing the same patient work - scan the code in chapter 13, or visit 5xyourwealth.com.au.

Contact Information

You can reach Victor Idoko at:

- *Email: victor@cfvadvisory.com.au*
- *Website: cfvadvisory.com.au*
- *LinkedIn: Victor Idoko*
- *Insta: cfvadvisory*
- *Tiktok: victoridokowlthadv*

Book a Meeting with Victor

calendly.com/cfvadvisory/financial-advice-introduction

www.ingramcontent.com/pod-product-compliance
Lightning Source LLC
LaVergne TN
LVHW050807061126
851857LV00012B/706
* 9 7 8 1 7 6 3 7 1 8 7 9 1 *